LITTLE

BOOK

OF

NOT

VERY

GOOD

RHYMES

LEE SMITH

Top Cat

As I sit out on the terrace

And soak up winter sun

I hear the blackbird singing

And think I might fancy one

But as I lift my head to move

He scuttles off so fast

So I recline back to the decking

And continue my repast

Off over the fence later

In through next doors' cat flap

Old Tiddles always leaves some food

Quite useful for a snack

Then I'll wind up Rex across the way

By walking by his window

He's very quick to bark

But when he runs he's very slow

Then its time to head off home

For evening son looms

Get fed and settled by the fire

And maybe me she'll groom

As in front of the fire

Upon her knee I lay

I'm thinking I'm a lucky cat

It's been a perfect day

A 7 year old at Christmas

My friends say Santa don't exist

So why would I believe

But I know that I saw him

In our lounge on Christmas eve

With big red coat and wellies

And white whiskers round his jaws

The only person that it could be

Is Santa Claus

He drank all mommy's sherry

And mince pies he ate 3

Then he delved into his sack

And placed some presents by the tree

He picked up all the carrots

Then vanished in a"poof"

Then I saw out the window

A carrot top fall off the roof

So to me it's extra special

The morn of Christmas day

Opening my presents

From Santa in his sleigh

Theirs To Serve

No chip of stone nor ink of pen
Can describe the fate of them
Their service given, so much more
Than their country ever thanked them for
Some came home, and some could not
Their families forced to bear the shock
Those that returned with injury
Tried so much more than you or me
To build themselves a better life
Always for the stars to strife
Though our hero don't expect
Accolades in retrospect
Theirs was not to be, as hero told
Their service for a common goal
To keep their country safe from harm
To rise up when we raise alarm
There not a thing a man could say
To make them flinch or turn away
From doing what they needed to
To make it safe for me and you
For you and I can never know
What it is to be hero

Fostering

Six years into our marriage my wife declared to me
If you would like it too, foster carers we can be
Our kids are now at nursery and I'm not one to shirk
But I'd rather be here for them than go back out to work
I've filled out all the forms and all you have to do
Is be there to support me and attend a course or two
The social worker came to visit, and upon that day
I rounded all sharp corners, and put the bleach away
"you may not prove suitable" the woman she opined
I said "if you don't want us then some other carers find"
The offer's there for us to take children one or two
Whether we are needed is entirely up to you
When the social worker left the wife was in a huff
She said "don't you say anything, I think you've said enough"
They probably won't want us now because of what you said
I had planned a lovely tea, but you can get your own instead
After many months had passed, a letter they did send
To help with our approval there were courses to attend
We went to all the courses on the paper they had put
And on my wife's instruction, my mouth stayed firmly shut
It became apparent that quite well we had been fairing
Approval came, and we began a life of Foster caring
More than one hundred kids have come to us since that day
And we have done what we can to help them on their way
I must admit throughout the years there have been 1 or 2
Who for, in spite of our efforts, there was little we could do
But still they come through our doors some are frail, others crying
That is what Foster carers are for
You never fail 'til you stop trying

Time Moves On

Will it ever be the same again for you and me

As it was way back when we were 21 and 23

We don't seem to have the spring of step that we enjoyed

When I chased all the girls, and you got all the boys

We don't seem to have the energy we had

Though we're not surprised, we are a little sad

There is so much more left for us to do

For, though we're tired and weary

We can still plough on through

One thing we have learnt throughout our generation

Is that, though it may be hard, we have determination

Age is just a number past which we can all go

Fuelled by adrenalin and a boundless ego

The sound ones strain to keep up, our vigour they just curse

I can go on for ages, with the assistance of my nurse

So no, it will never be the same, neither should it be

For we did some crazy things when we were young and we were free

We are now much better placed to enjoy lives we never had

With fancy cars, and meals out, and trips to Trinidad

Little Things

I'm looking at the queen's
Birthday honours list
And once again it seems
That off it I've been missed
I wonder what it is this year
That I have done wrong
When other people get
But I don't deserve a gong
I may not be a sportsman
Or a stage celebrity
I haven't climbed a mountain
I can't even climb a tree
But I thought I might get something
For my contribution to
All those little things
That nobody wants to do
Now I'm getting worried
Because our queen is getting old
She probably won't remember me
And I'll be left out in the cold

Mortal Pain

There's a man I know at work
Though his wife I've never met
It seems that she has cancer
And the lad is so upset
"They say she just has days to go
Or hopefully some weeks"
And as he tells me this
I see a tear run down his cheek
They were childhood sweethearts
And children they have three
They've rarely had a cross word
And never fail to agree
To see this mountain of a man
Stand with me as he wept
Exhausted by his care for her
For months he's barely slept
I curse the fact that for him
This upset I can't mend
For I know that though his wife will pass
His pain will never end.

Reward for a year

Oh Santa Claus please come to me
And leave a present by my tree
All this year I have been good
I've milked the cows and chopped the wood
I've carted corn and made the hay
I've counted ewes and lambs at play
I've fed the pigs and mucked them out
I've worked through snow and rain and drought
To see a little present there
Will let me know that someone cares
Will fill me full of Christmas cheer
Will help me through another year
It doesn't matter what you bring
I'd be pleased with anything
To farm and field from Santa's sleigh
I hope for something Christmas Day

In remembrance

From Cornish beach to highland tower

In silence at eleventh hour

In honour of those gone before

Who gave their lives in times of war

Surrounded by the poppies red

We mourn the passing of the dead

The men of air and land and sea

Who knew of pride and chivalry

Who's bravery and courage bold

Mean that they will ne'er grow old

Hewn from rock and cast to fen

Forever, we remember them

Remember Them

Tell me, will you remember them
The men who passed through here
The ones who entered firefight
Whilst choking down their fear
Those who fought for regiment
Rank of foe, forced to divide
Though many may have fallen
Not one stepped aside
For those returning from the fray
In state of injury
Who may have lost a body part
But keep their dignity
Who's bravery and courage
Knew no bounds at all
Who's maxim was keep fighting for the cause
Unless you fall
Most of us will never see
The searing desert haze
The firefight in a Kirkuk night
Or Kandahari days
Remember these brave soldiers
A hero every one
Who met their fate in biting rain
Or under scorching sun

Flander's Field

With petals red, remember me

As I am far across the sea

Of poppies in a Flanders field

Though I fell, I did not yield

In fields of war the poppy grows

It's blood red flower reflecting those

Who fought for King, and so much more

Those brave young men who went to war

Whenever you a poppy see

In Flanders field, remember me

Nature's Summer

Meadowsweet and fumitory

Marigold and cow parsley

Mayweed nettle and daisy fair

The smell of summer fills the air

Foxes run and rabbits gambol

Cattle graze and people ramble

Picnic in the woods by day

All the children run and play

The sun shines down on all below

The summer we have come to know

See reflections in the river

Eels below through reed-beds slither

Kingfisher dives in to attack

Returning with a stickleback

Heron strutting in the mud

Gulping down a tiny Chubb

Babbling brook and birdsong sound

The wonder of nature all around

Father's Advice

In the ante room on wedding day

Father to his daughter said

Don't let those thoughts of fear

Get inside your head

I'll walk you down the aisle

Then your vows you will exchange

Then everyone will sing a hymn

Of that there's nothing strange

In order to remember this

And to sustain her vim

As she walked she chanted out the words

Aisle, change, hymn

Holiday

I'm sitting on the sun-bed
Upsoaking winter sun
Reflecting on my holiday
And the things I could have done
I could have done pilates
Or rode a mountain bike
Played beach volleyball
Or joined a morning hike
Played tennis, spun or windsurfed
On the sea so blue
But none of the above
Are what I chose to do
I lay out on the sun-bed
Then had a little swim
The pool at first is cold
But it's alright once you're in
I walk along the beach
With my lover hand in hand
And watch the tide behind us
Wash our footsteps from the sand
I watch the chipmunks play
With the pigeons in the dunes
Then amble to the pool bar
For a drink and banging tunes
I sizzle in the sunshine
And turn from white to red
Then wish I hadn't done it
When I'm rolling in my bed

Gradually the tan comes
But the body isn't there
Not so much Adonis
As a bloody big brown bear
Maybe I've not spent it
In the way you would have done
But it's up to me how I do
My fortnight in the sun

It could happen

The vegemites have got their way

Us stockmen we have had our day

Vegetables is what we eat

Nowadays there is no meat

You're allowed to have courgette bake

But not fresh lamb or juicy steak

No breakfast bacon from a pig

Instead there's cereal , juice or fig

On Monday morn I see my mate

Jailed for pheasant on his plate

At lunch I stare down at my dish

And wish we could at least have fish

The cows now from the yard are gone

The slurry pit a home for swan

Silent bar the pigeons coo

No sheep to baa, no cows to moo

Where we can't grow corn or harvest maize

Badgers with the horses graze

At least electricity is cheap

Made from the stuff not fit to eat

So off to the petting farm we go

To see the beast we used to know

It's the only place you'll find them now

Since demise of horn and rise of plough

The Foster Tree

When you look up at the moon
Do you think of me
Rooted in my field alone
I, the foster tree
Those in need they come to me
And stand beneath the foster tree
Though their lives be tossed and torn
I give them shelter from the storm
In scorching sun in need of aid
My canopy can offer shade
Singing in the branches see
The children of the foster tree

Man or Dragon?

I'm an independent woman and I don't "need" a man
Not one to tell me what to do for I know who I am
I don't want one who expects his tea
When he walks in the door
Or doesn't want me to be a free spirit anymore
I want one who can love me for simple being me
One who when I'm feeling ill will bring me a cup of tea
Who makes me smile and makes me sing and on the eye is easy
One who doesn't sleep around and wants to be with me
One who has hid own mind does the things he wants to do
Who recognises that, I am a person too
Someone I miss when I am out at work
Someone who will never a promise to me shirk
Will I ever meet him
I wonder when or how
When I told this to my genie
He said, what colour dragon now?

My Nutty Friend

A friend of mine has passed away
Pongo was his name
Whatever you were playing
He would be there for a game
Whether in the park
The garden, or the hall
He would join you for a meal
Pr the throwing of a ball
He would give you lot's of fuss
When you came home in the hail
He could even clear the table
With the swishing of his tail
Without my spotty, dotty friend
Life will never be the same
The tin man of the doggy world
Pongo was his name

Keeping Safe

Please stay in, don't go out

There's a nasty bug about

It could knock you down and make you ill

It could land you in the hospital

Your temperature could rise so high

It's possible that you might die

If you survive you still don't know

If you'll be fit and good to go

If you stay in and do your bit

And all those around stop spreading it

Pretty soon we'll all be out

And say, what was all the fuss about

We'll live our lives once again

Though probably in a different vein

Misdirected

Is it a plane, is it a bird

No, it's New Year and that's Mr Absurd

Who this year is resolute

To ditch the cake and eat the fruit

Become a member of the gym

Where he can exercise and swim

The first few visits seem quite hard

But he's determined to lose that lard

But what took 10 years to put on

Will not fall off in just week one

His legs will ache and body tire

His pulse will race and he'll perspire

Shower, change then in the car

Raid the glovebox for Mars bars

Week six he to the gym returns

To fight the fat and feel the burn

Rowing and swimming for all his worth

But can't reduce his massive girth

One day he'll maybe see his hips

If he could only leave out the fish & chips

By now you will have guessed

That I'm Mr Absurd

Yes, I'm the one who ate the pies

And all the lemon curd

I'm the one who is too big

To fit on all those gadgets

One who believes the towels and showers

Are only made for midgets

Arthritic man who finds so hard the lifting of a leg
The only sit-up I can do is sitting up in bed
After a gym session , I may feel like I'm dying
One day I may lose some weight
You never fail, 'til you stop trying

Tender Skip

Tender is the heart
that beats inside my breast
It beats when I am busy
And it beats when I'm at rest
But as if I'd jumped out of a plane
And fell ten thousand feet
When I look at you, my love
My poor heart skips a beat
It did it when I met you
It does it every day
Not in forty years
Has this feeling gone away
For, though I carry too much weight
And moan about my legs and hips
Every time I see your face
There's part of me that skips

Be Me

It's ok not to be ok
To feel that you can't face the day
To dread the thought of new sunrise
To find it hard to be outside
It's ok too to conjure up
Your courage from a coffee cup
It's ok too to not compete
But just try hard to be complete
It's ok just to sit a while
And read this rhyme
And maybe smile
It's ok too to turn around
And decide to go to town
It's always ok to be yourself
To look after your mental health
Whatever you may choose today
I pray that you will be
OK

The Farmer's Day

There's a cow that needs calving

A tree down across the dyke

There's water in the workshop

It was raining in the night

All within five minutes

Of stepping out the door

With all the things to do today

I don't need any more

So, first job is the calving

It just needed a tug

Then in the workshop a bucket

Until the hole is plugged

The tree can stay for now

Although it's acting like a dam

First things first

I must give the beast their bread and jam

It's coming down in torrents now

I'm getting soaking wet

Although I've got my hat and coat on

It still goes down my neck

All are fed and watered

Calves are bedded down

The new one is now up

And follows mum around

She stops up in the corner

And baby latches on

Suckling with tail wagging

For now my work is done

Into the house for breakfast

And plan the rest of day

How to mend the roof

And drag the tree away

Although there's some work done

There's lots more left to do

Sheep to move

And beast to come from pen 1 into 2

The list goes on and on

It ends I know not when

Then I'll get up tomorrow morning

And do it all again

Keep The Home Fires Burning

With my kit on my shoulder
And a smile on my face
I won't be sorry to leave that place
I've done my stint
And home I go
To the girl I love in Walthamstow

You're heading home Billy
Tommy's coming too
Now we've all done
The job we came to do
You'll be there before me
You'll land in time for tea
Tell them all in Blighty
To save a cup for me

I'd bring them all home
If I could
But there's only me
Left in the wood
The others in the field they lay
Brave men one and all were they
Their memory will stay with me
Their courage and their bravery
Across the field
Past church and tower
They lie in a sea of poppy flower

Live and Let Live

An omnivore is what I am

I love Chicken, pork and beef and lamb

Each night I sit and join the feast

To honour farmer and the beast

There are those who don't want to eat

My creamy fish or juicy meat

To them I say, just feel free

But don't come to my house for tea

I don't presume to tell you what to eat

So don't tell me I can't eat meat

There's room for both of us on earth

We should recognise each other's worth

You eat the veg, I'll eat the meat

Then both our lives will be complete

Opportunity passed

Guess who it was

As summertime was ending

Woke up right on time

Even though he wasn't working

Made a cup of tea

And as he took a sip

Suddenly thought

I am a stupid git

The clock should have been put back an hour

The thought that I forgot

Ha turned a good day sour

To get my extra hour kip

I'll have to wait another year

And knowing my luck

I'll be working then I fear

Who Wins?

Is it the one who scores most goals

Or puts the ball into the hole

Is it the first to cross the line

Or brew award winning wine

Is it the fastest round the track

Or first to the North Pole and back

Is it the one who baked a cake

Or was the best at lifting weights

Is it the one who can mountain climb

Or run a mile in record time

It's a feeling that we all desire

To stand upon the rostrum higher

But winning is that inner drive

To achieve and stay alive

To try each day to be our best

To work hard, play hard, 'til we rest

Whether gaining pace or getting thinner

Everyone can be a winner

Poppy Peace

Remember those who did not yield
Lying in the poppy field
Those who saw in battles glow
Defiantly the poppy grow
Pierced by black it's petals red
Reflect the blood spilt of the dead
Tell me will you remember me
If I look up and poppies see
To see them high above my head
In the breeze their flowers red
I both pride and sorrow feel
Out there in the poppy field

I'm Just Saying

Come in from the rain

Feel the fire lights warmth and glow

Come and share a coffee with these good folk that you know

Talk about the good times

And tell them all your worries

They'll sit and listen quietly

There is no need to hurry

Have a good old moan

Get it all off your chest

Then sit and laugh and joke about the things that you love best

Though we can't control the weather

And the struggle never ends

All of us can learn to talk

There's nowt as good as friends

1917

He joins the line
The whistle blows
Then, over the top he goes
Beside him bugler sounds his call
Then down into the mud he falls
Stifled now his battle note
A bullet piercing through his throat
Ten thousand men, maybe more
Stumble through the mud and gore
Baying guns and howling shell
Turn Passchendaele to living hell
Whistling past, that one was close
Destined for our Captain Oakes
Another of the great and good
Lying face down in the mud
In foxhole now and bayonet fixed
Dispatch grenades, then join the mix
Driving on, we must not fail
This cold wet morn in Passchendaele

Printed in Great Britain
by Amazon

32670987R00020

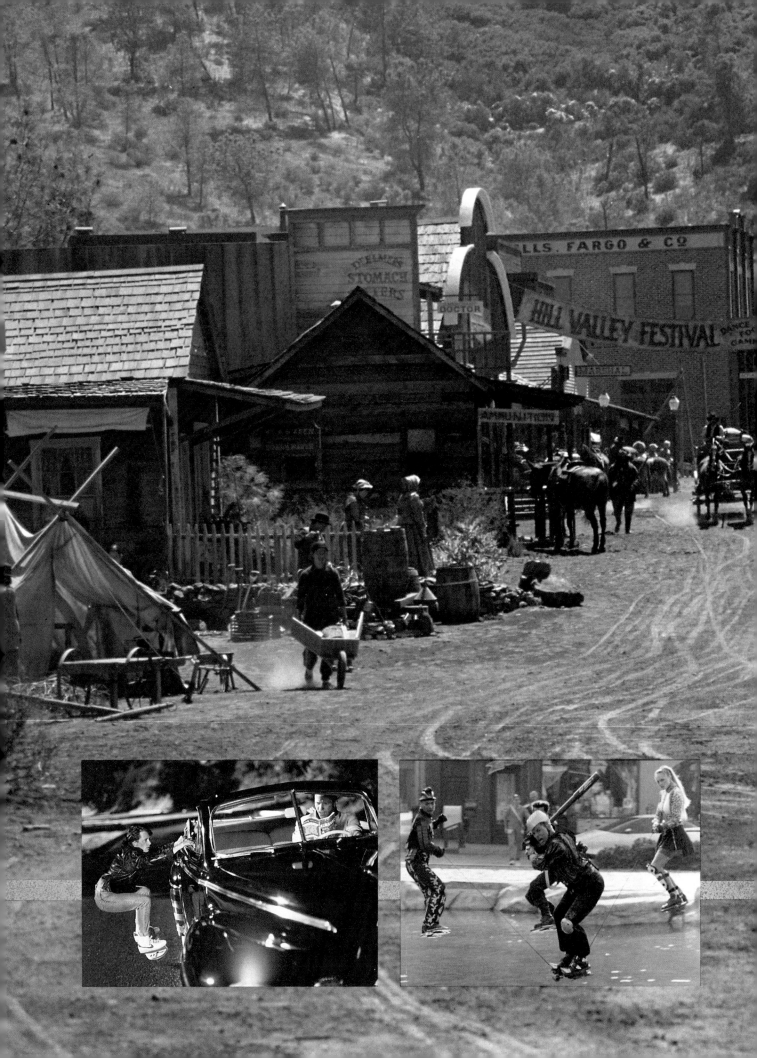

BACK TO THE FUTURE™

THE OFFICIAL BOOK OF THE COMPLETE MOVIE TRILOGY

MICHAEL KLASTORIN
AND SALLY HIBBIN

HAMLYN

Photographic acknowledgments
Poster artwork by Drew Struzan Illustrations Inc
All photographs by
Ralph Nelson Jr. and Jane O'Neal

Back to the Future
Based on a screenplay by
Robert Zemeckis & Bob Gale
Back to the Future Part II
Based on a screenplay by Bob Gale
Story by Robert Zemeckis & Bob Gale
Back to the Future Part III
Based on a screenplay by Bob Gale
Story by Robert Zemeckis & Bob Gale

Designed by Kit Johnson

Published in 1990
by The Hamlyn Publishing Group
Limited, a division of
The Octopus Publishing Group,
Michelin House, 81 Fulham Road,
London SW3 6RB

ISBN 0 600 57031 2

Printed in Great Britain

CONTENTS

FOREWORD

No one can predict the future.

And in 1980, when we first conceived Back to the Future *we never would have predicted that it would take four years to get the project off the ground.*

Or that the finished movie would become one of the biggest hits of all time.

Or that it would lead to not one but two sequels, comprising a movie trilogy that, worldwide, will eventually do roughly a billion dollars' worth of business.

Or that the title itself would become a catch-phrase in the English language, used by Presidents Reagan and Bush in speeches promising to take America 'back to the future'.

Or that we'd be writing the introduction to a book about the history of the whole thing.

But maybe that's why everyone finds the future so fascinating: you never know what it's going to be.

We certainly didn't.

Or, as Doctor Emmett Brown said about the future in Part II, *'Well, that's all in the past.'*

Robert Zemeckis and Bob Gale

THE MAKING OF
BACK
TO FUTURE
THE

DIRECTOR ROBERT ZEMECKIS and screenwriter Bob Gale had always hoped to make a movie about time travel, a subject that had fascinated them both since childhood. When Gale returned home to visit his parents in St. Louis after the filming of Used Cars (1980), he made what would turn out to be a significant discovery – his father's high school yearbook. As he thumbed through the pages, he began to wonder what it would have been like to go to school with his father. Would they have been friends with many of the same interests, or would they have had nothing in common and dislike each other on sight? When Gale mentioned this premise to Zemeckis, he too became excited with the possibilities, and thus was born the story of Marty McFly, the 17-year-old who travels back through time to meet his parents as teenagers.

GENESIS

'It's about a kid who goes back in time, meets his parents, and his mother falls in love with him.'

This one sentence was the starting point for a motion picture trilogy that would span the course of five years in production, and captivate millions of moviegoers around the world. This was, of course, the development pitch for the original *Back to the Future* (1985).

Zemeckis and Gale took their fledgling project to Columbia Pictures, the studio that had produced their last film. 'It was an easy pitch,' recalls Bob Gale. 'Frank Price, the head of the studio, was excited by the concept. Bob Zemeckis kept explaining specific scenes that we had thought of, and I kept leaning over, whispering to him that he had said enough. I knew we had it.' They were given a script development deal by Columbia in September 1980, and delivered the first draft in April 1981. But Columbia passed on the project. According to Gale, 'They thought it was a really nice, cute, warm film, but just not raunchy enough. They suggested that we take it to Disney.'

After making the rounds of other studios who echoed Columbia's sentiments, they did exactly that. They took it to Disney. Unfortunately, once there, they were told that a film which featured a

director to get work. Moreover, they were also concerned that Spielberg's reputation might suffer if *Back to the Future* didn't prove to be a success. That situation would soon change.

Zemeckis, depressed and frustrated at the inability to get *Back to the Future* into production, decided he would instead direct the first good script he was offered. That script came from producer (and star) Michael Douglas, and Zemeckis had his first certified box-office smash in *Romancing the Stone* (1984). In a town where it's said that you're only as good as your last picture, Robert Zemeckis was suddenly hot and studios that had once turned him down now approached him and Bob Gale about making *Back to the Future*. Mulling over the offers, the pair decided to go with the person who had always been enthusiastic from the start — Steven Spielberg. *Back to the Future* was a 'go'!

As the film headed into pre-production, all concerned felt the addition of a second producer to work with Bob Gale would benefit the project. Executive producer Frank Marshall suggested Neil Canton, with whom he had worked many times since 1971 on *What's Up, Doc?* Canton read the script, met with Zemeckis and Gale, and the team was complete.

◄*Marty McFly (Michael J. Fox) wakes up in the year 1955, to find himself face to face with the 17-year-old girl who will ultimately become his mother (Lea Thompson).*

mother falling in love with her son, no matter what the circumstances, was not quite traditional family fare, and a bit too *risqué* to be made under the Disney banner.

There was one producer in Hollywood who was very interested in *Back to the Future* — Steven Spielberg. Spielberg had been the executive producer of *I Wanna Hold Your Hand* (1978) and *Used Cars*, and Zemeckis and Gale had collaborated on the screenplay of Spielberg's *1941* (1979). Although there was a great temptation to ally themselves again with Spielberg, to get their film made, Zemeckis and Gale were hesitant. Since none of their previous films together had been box-office successes, Zemeckis and Gale worried about gaining a reputation of being no more than protégés of Spielberg, dependent upon the

Asked the biggest problem he was faced with when given the task of directing *Back to the Future*, Bob Zemeckis remembers: 'We had relatively little money. We had to make an enormous film on a limited budget as well as a limited time schedule, and make it the best we could.' The film was finished within weeks of its release, with the sound effects for the 70mm prints added a mere 24 hours before the first show for the general public.

While in production, no one connected with the film had any idea that the movie they were making would prove to be a smash hit. 'It was only in the first sneak preview,' says Zemeckis, 'that we realized we had something special. The audience loved it, and their reaction was beyond our wildest expectations. Up until that point, it was anyone's guess.'

GOING BACK TO
BACK TO THE FUTURE

In its release, *Back to the Future* proved to be an enormous success, grossing over $350 million worldwide, making it one of the biggest box-office movies of all time. Letters poured in to the filmmakers from all over the world asking for a sequel.

When Universal Pictures approached Zemeckis and Gale about the possibility of continuing the adventures of Marty and Doc, the pair were amenable to the idea, but only if the original cast agreed to return as well. Both Michael J. Fox and Christopher Lloyd agreed to return, as long as Zemeckis, Gale and Canton were involved, and *Back to the Future Part II* was up and running.

As Zemeckis and Gale set out to fashion the story that Gale would eventually turn into the screenplay for *Part II*, they realized that they would have to start where *Part I* left off: with Doc returning from the future announcing, 'It's your kids, Marty! Something's got to be done about your kids!'

'When we made *Back to the Future*, the original ending was merely a joke,' explains Bob Gale. 'No one had any thoughts of a sequel at the time, and we figured it was appropriate for the heroes to go flying into the proverbial sunset and off to a new adventure. When we began the outline for *Part II*, we knew we'd have to start at that point because of all the letters we'd received. With so many people having seen the first film, we couldn't not pay off the promise. It wouldn't have been fair to all the fans of the original film.'

What neither Gale nor Zemeckis realized at the time they were formulating the second film was that they had a surplus of material, and didn't know what to cut from their story. 'It was then,' says Gale, 'that we made a good news/bad news phone call to Universal. "The bad news,"' they explained to the executives, '"is that we can't make *Back to the Future Part II* for the summer of 1989. The good news is that we'll have *Part II* for Thanksgiving and *Back to the Future Part III* for the summer after that." I think,' recalls Gale, 'when we made that call, they thought we were kidding.' They weren't.

WORDS AND PICTURES

◄ In 1985 Michael J. Fox and Bob Zemeckis take their first trip 'Back to the Future'.

'Bob and I both come from middle-class families in the mid-West, and have the same tastes in movies – both of us leaning towards films that intrigue, involve, and most of all, entertain.'

BOB GALE

For Bob Zemeckis and Bob Gale, the *Back to the Future* trilogy has been a true collaboration. They co-wrote the first film, and on *Part II* and *Part III* Zemeckis and Gale conceived the story, with Gale writing the screenplays. Their ability to work together is a result of their similar backgrounds, sensibilities and sense of humour.

After they establish their premise, Zemeckis and

▼ As the three movies cover a multitude of time periods and changes, Gale keeps a bulletin board in his office, covered with index cards, showing the progression of the adventures. The cards are also used as reference for scenes under revision.

▲ After Bob Gale makes his changes in the script, the revised pages are printed on different-coloured paper to reflect the date of the changes. The original shooting script of Part III was printed on blue paper. When the production wrapped, only two original blue pages remained untouched.

Gale work on specific scenes for the story, noting them on index cards. That process is rarely done in a continuous order, as many scenes dictate necessary action in previous ones.

'We're great believers in the "set it up/pay it off" school of writing,' says Gale. 'For instance, in order to have Marty "invent" rock and roll in 1955, it must be established that he knows how to play the guitar in 1985. Because we wanted to have Marty play "Johnny B. Goode" at the dance, we knew we needed a scene in the beginning of the film, where he auditions his band at the high school.'

Bob Zemeckis gives another example of how one joke led to an important creative decision. 'When Marty first arrives in 1955, we wanted the farm family to mistake the time machine for a flying saucer. We searched for the appropriate vehicle, and found that the DeLorean's gull wing doors and overall design gave it the resemblance of a spaceship. The DeLorean became our time machine.'

The writing process is never final. A script passes through several drafts before the cameras roll, and it changes throughout the filming as well. The very first draft of the Back to the Future script was vastly different from the final product – Marty was originally a streetwise video pirate ('The studio refused to let us make a film where the hero was a video pirate,' explains Zemeckis); Doc had a pet monkey instead of a dog; the time machine was not a car, but resembled a refrigerator ('We were concerned that kids would accidentally lock themselves in refrigerators'); and Doc gets the power to return Marty to 1985 by taking the time machine to the site of an A-bomb test in the Nevada desert ('It was too expensive to go on location').

Zemeckis is a perfectionist, both during the shooting of the film and in post-production. 'He's never finished with an idea. From the moment he gets up in the morning, he's thinking how to make it better,' observes first assistant director David McGiffert. 'He's like an artist who retouches his picture, even when it's hanging in the gallery.' Director of photography Dean Cundey agrees. 'The production of any Bob Zemeckis film can be called difficult. He's tenacious and relentless to achieve the final product as he envisions it. That's what also makes any Robert Zemeckis film an event.'

BOB GALE / NEIL CANTON

CO-PRODUCERS

▲ *Bob Gale (l.) and Neil Canton (r.) have produced all three* Back to the Futures, *overseeing every aspect of the productions from preproduction to the films' release.*

'I caught the filmmaking bug at high school in St. Louis,' says Bob Gale, where he participated in a senior class tradition – the making of a 16mm movie. From high school, Gale attended New Orleans' Tulane University, where he majored in engineering 'because when you're from Missouri, the idea of going into movies is pretty crazy.' After his first semester, the idea seemed a bit less crazy, and he applied to the film school of the University of Southern California. In his first year there he befriended a classmate named Bob Zemeckis.

Gale aspired to write, and Zemeckis to direct, so they combined their talents. Together they wrote *1941, I Wanna Hold Your Hand* and *Used Cars*. Gale also got his first producing credits during this time, initially as the associate producer on *I Wanna Hold Your Hand* and as the producer of *Used Cars*. While Zemeckis was directing *Romancing the Stone*, Gale wrote and produced a TV pilot based on *Used Cars*. He has produced (with Neil Canton) and written all three *Back to the Futures*. Following the release of *Part III*, Gale hopes to take some time off, and then plans to 'try my hand at directing. There are two screenplays I've written that I'd like to get off the ground.'

Neil Canton was born and raised in New York City, and graduated from American University in Washington, D.C. He studied government in college, and was exposed to the film industry through his father, a prominent entertainment executive. After spending one summer in California working on a film, he decided to remain in Los Angeles permanently, choosing production as his intended career. 'I was hooked.'

His first job in the motion picture industry was that of assistant to director Peter Bogdanovich on *What's Up, Doc?* and they continued that association over the course of four films, including *Paper Moon* (1973) and *Nickelodeon* (1976). He spent two years on Orson Welles' long-awaited *The Other Side of the Wind*, and worked with Walter Hill on *The Warriors* (1979). Canton produced the cult favourite *The Adventures of Buckaroo Banzai* (1984) (which co-starred Christopher Lloyd) before his first meeting with Gale and Zemeckis. Of that meeting, he recalls, 'It felt like a very natural relationship that I had always been a part of.' In between *Back to the Future Part I* and *Part II*, Canton produced the hit comedy *The Witches of Eastwick* (1987).

ROBERT ZEMECKIS
DIRECTOR

▼ Four years after their first adventure, Michael J. Fox and Bob Zemeckis team up again for Back to the Future Part II. 'I would not have agreed to do the sequels unless Bob was directing,' says Fox.

Born in Chicago, Bob Zemeckis began making 8mm films in high school. He attended Northern Illinois University before transferring to USC's film school where he met Bob Gale. One day, at Universal Pictures, Zemeckis's class was introduced to a young director named Steven Spielberg.

Zemeckis asked Spielberg to look at the student film that Zemeckis had directed. The film, *Field of Honor*, which won an Academy Award, impressed Spielberg, and he helped Zemeckis and Gale obtain a development deal for an original screenplay. They wrote *1941*, which Spielberg later directed. 'I feel that every film Zemeckis and Gale have made,' says Spielberg, 'has been on a high order of pop cultural art — something that I don't think many other filmmakers are tapping into.'

Zemeckis made his directorial debut with *I Wanna Hold Your Hand*, a story about a group of teenagers trying to meet the Beatles during their first visit to America, and followed it with *Used Cars*. His third film, *Romancing the Stone*, proved to be the turning point in his career, and its success afforded him the opportunity to direct another project he had co-written with Bob Gale — *Back to the Future*. The film was the highest-grossing movie of 1985, and further served to enhance Zemeckis's reputation as one of the top directors in the film industry. He spent the next two years perfecting a process to effectively blend live action with animated 'Toons', and received even greater acclaim as the director of 1988's top-grossing movie, *Who Framed Roger Rabbit?*

Zemeckis has spent over two years in the production and distribution of the *Back to the Future* sequels, and plans to take an immediate and extended vacation. 'Having been immersed in the world of *Back to the Future* for so many years, I need to take some time, clear my brain, recharge the batteries, live life a bit, and see what happens.'

BOB'S VISION

(AS TOLD BY THE CAST AND CREW)

'If you leap for the moon, you might land on the roof.'

BOB ZEMECKIS

'You always plan more than you can possibly do,' says Zemeckis of his approach to filmmaking. 'We put in much more than is necessary and then it all shakes out in the actual production, finding what can and can't be done. If you start to compromise at the very beginning, nobody's going to let you add to it later.

'The films I like to make are stories that are unique to the cinema, stories that not only record life but in fact are larger than life, and can be best told on a giant screen rather than in an opera or novel or any other arena. That's where all the special effects, moving camera shots, wild characters and humour come together. If you had to categorize what I do, I guess you'd call me an action/adventure/comedy/suspense/special-effects/mass-popular-culture-style director. It's a good thing I don't have to have business cards printed. They'd cost a fortune.'

'Bob's so innovative, he's deceptive,' explains David McGiffert. 'He exudes calmness when all hell is breaking loose, and has the greatest quality a director can have. He inspires tremendous loyalty in the cast and crew.'

'We know exactly what the other needs,' says Michael J. Fox. 'We have a kind of shorthand, which is a wonderful relationship for an actor to have with a director. I trust him completely. If anyone else asked me to do the things that he's asked of me, I'd probably call my agent and have him get me the hell out of there. Bob has, at times, asked me to do enormously exaggerated moves and facial contortions that go against every instinct I have as an actor. But when he does, I know it's part of the plan, and I've never been disappointed with the results.'

'One of the things that makes Bob my favourite director,' says director of photography Dean Cundey, 'is that he's totally dedicated to the film, with no ego problems getting in the way.' 'The story is the thing,' agrees Fox. 'It's not about Bob being a hero with the camera, or any of the actors being heroes with performances. It's about telling the story, exciting people and engaging them.'

'He solicits contributions and suggestions, and is not afraid to listen to anybody about anything,' says Dean Cundey. 'Bob embodies a most unique quality of being able to give specific direction, while also giving the cast and crew a sense of total freedom to contribute to the film's creation.'

'Having shot *Part II* and *Part III* back to back,' says Michael J. Fox, 'these people have been together for 11 months and I don't think there's a single person on this production who has a bad word to say about Bob.'

The rest of the cast concur with Fox. 'He's the smartest man I've ever met,' says Lea Thompson. 'He knows exactly what he wants and how to get it. You have to be a certain kind of actor to work with such a precise director. You have to trust him completely. Bob has never betrayed that trust or steered us wrong.' 'He enthuses you,' adds Christopher Lloyd, 'so you want to give him your best.' Thomas F. Wilson notes: 'He must have a hundred megabyte hard disk in his brain. I've never worked with anyone who has such a command of filmmaking, not only technically but in the dramatic sense as well. He has a sense for a scene — a sense of when a joke is needed and when it isn't, knowing exactly what will work for each character.'

TECHNICALITIES

Zemeckis never constructs a stationary frame. He likes to use wide lenses, often shooting with the camera on a crane or dolly, which creates a fluidity of motion and also gives the audience greater accessibility to the action.

'The technical side of filmmaking is something I've picked up over the years,' says Zemeckis, 'and it's a side I don't particularly care for. Making films is a time-consuming process which can strain your patience, especially when dealing with special effects. Setting up for them is like watching grass grow but they're necessary for movies like these. The reward is the way they finally turn out, and the amount of fun they provide in the finished product.'

After filming has been completed, that finished product is the result of months of painstaking work in post-production, where Zemeckis remains an intimate participant. Editors Artie Schmidt and Harry Keramidas reveal that the director makes

innumerable changes to his work, tightening the scenes in some places, reworking them in others. Says Keramidas: 'A Robert Zemeckis film is never final until there's an audience watching it in the theatre.'

▲▲ *Bob Zemeckis directs two veterans of western films – Dub Taylor (l.) and Harry Carey, Jr. – in the barroom sequence from Part III.*

◀ *The film crew position themselves on the train to film the sequence where the DeLorean is pushed into time travel by 'steam power'.*

▲ *Bob Zemeckis watches the day's video rushes with various members of the production team.*

THE SPACE-TIME CONTINUUM

1885

1955

1

8

2

9

7

STARTING IN 1985-1

1. Marty goes to 1955.

2. Marty changes history in 1955, goes back to 1985-2, in which George is a success instead of a wimp.

3. Doc takes Marty and Jennifer to 2015.

4. Old Biff steals DeLorean, goes to 1955, gives himself the Almanac.

5. Old Biff returns to 2015.

6. Doc and Marty and Jennifer go back to Biffhorrific 1985–A.

7. Doc and Marty go to 1955 to retrieve the Almanac.

8. Marty goes back to 1885 to rescue Doc.

9. Marty returns to 1985-2.

LEGEND

BTTF · 1

BTTF · 2

BTTF · 3

THE FIVE FACES OF MICHAEL J. FOX

MICHAEL J. FOX was everyone's first choice to portray Marty McFly. 'We had all seen Michael on Family Ties,' says producer Neil Canton, 'and we knew that he was adept at comedy, but it's more than that.' Adds Robert Zemeckis, 'He does have great comedy timing, but what's more important is that he embodies an "everyman" quality. You feel comfortable going on this adventure with Michael.'

Michael was first given the script to *Back to the Future* in the midst of his third season on *Family Ties*. 'The script for the original film,' says Fox, 'was the complete movie-going experience. It had

MICHAEL'S McFLYS

'He makes my dialogue sound better than I ever thought it could.'

BOB GALE

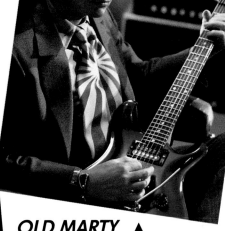

MARTY ▶

'Marty,' says Michael, 'is our guide through the world of time travel. We see the action through his eyes, tapping into his sense of awe and amazement.' Marty McFly is just an ordinary teenager, who, like so many others, dreams of being a rock star.

His relationship with Doc Brown is what takes him into his unusual adventures. 'If George McFly had always been the successful, self-assured author he becomes at the end of Part I,' theorizes Fox, 'Marty would never have had the relationship he has with Doc. The Doc is the kind of positive and intriguing father influence/role model that Marty needs.'

Marty also has an Achilles' heel, as we learn in Part II. That weakness is his pride and defensiveness: 'Nobody calls me "Chicken!!"' 'That is the chink in his armour of innocence,' says Fox. 'He's a nice guy, and in Part II, he's learning that it's difficult to be a nice guy. The added dimensions of the character in the sequels make me glad I established so much of him in the first film. He's just a kid, and it's

fun to play someone with a lack of experience as opposed to a lack of intelligence. Five years later, it's a bit more of an acting challenge to find a way to wipe out my acquired worldliness and prejudgement, and return to the role.'

OLD MARTY ▲

In the year 2015, Jennifer and Doc get a look at Marty at the age of 47. The years have not been kind to our hero. At 17, he was in an auto accident which damaged his hand, and thwarted his ambitions of a career in music. He has grown up disillusioned and unfulfilled. Life does not hold much promise for this Marty, but he still holds on to his misguided pride. 'For personal reasons,' says Michael, who lost his father during the shoot, 'I especially enjoyed playing Old Marty. There's a lot of my father in him – a gruffness that obviously concealed genuine sweetness, and a deep desire for everything to be all right.'

every element I look for when either watching or acting in a comedy.' Arrangements were made seemingly overnight. 'One minute I'm reading the script,' recalls Michael, 'and the next thing I know, it's 3am, and I'm in a parking lot with Chris Lloyd, a dog and a DeLorean.'

From mid-January to mid-March of 1985, a typical day in the life of Michael J. Fox meant reporting to Paramount studios for the TV show from 10am to 6pm, and then on to Universal for *Back to the Future* chores from approximately 6.30pm to 2.30am. Fridays were even more hectic, as *Family Ties* taped in front of a live audience on Friday evenings. Fox would rehearse with his TV family from noon until 5pm, perform two tapings of the show, and then report to the *Back to the Future* set at 10pm. The motion picture

crew would then film until 6 or 7 the following morning, leaving the actor a shortened weekend to recuperate, only to start the routine all over again on Monday morning. 'It was difficult, but exhilarating,' says Michael of the experience. 'I wanted to work as much as I could at the time, and there was enough similarity between Alex Keaton and Marty McFly to make the transition easy, and enough differences to make it interesting. There were times, however, when I literally had drivers come to my apartment, get me out of bed, point me toward the shower, put a shirt and pants on the bed, and get me ready to go.' When plans for the

watched movies like **Foxes** *(1980)* and **Little Darlings** *(1980)*, and had the physical and emotional attitude and rhythm perfectly set in my mind. When the time came to put on the dress and high heels, though, I suddenly found myself embarrassed standing in front of a crew that I had been working with for years.'

'I think the hardest part about Marlene,' says Fox, 'is that the audience had to accept her as a normal teenage girl, even though I was playing her. Usually, when you see a man dressed as a woman – say, for instance, on **Monty Python** – part of the joke is that you understand it's really a man in a dress. I didn't have the luxury of being able to "wink" at the audience.'

MARTY JUNIOR ▲

Martin McFly Jr. is the reason Doc and Marty make their journey to the future. Although he physically resembles Marty, his demeanour is reminiscent of the easily intimidated George McFly of 1955. As Marty watches his son ruthlessly bullied by Griff in the Cafe '80s, his worst fears are realized – 'He's a complete wimp!'

MARLENE ▶

Michael loved the idea of playing Marty's daughter in the future. 'I talked to all the women in my life,

SEAMUS ▲

Seamus is Marty's great-great-grandfather, an Irish farmer who emigrated to Hill Valley in the late 1800s. 'Seamus,' says Fox, 'has learned through experience that one can have pride without a fall, that in fact pride can steer you away from a fall, and he tries to impart this knowledge to Marty.'

Both Michael and Lea Thompson (who plays Seamus's wife Maggie) spent time with a dialogue coach to perfect their Irish accent. 'The dialect was a bitch,' recalls Michael. 'You think you have a handle on the accent, and then you sit down with a dialogue coach who tells you you've got it wrong.'

sequel were being made, Michael was so delighted with the prospect of returning to play Marty McFly that he went back to those very same working conditions he had gone through four years earlier. There was, however, one major difference that Fox had not encountered during the filming of the first feature. As if filming a motion picture and the final season of his television show weren't enough, Fox also had the added but welcome distraction of the imminent arrival of his and actress Tracy Pollan's first child. Fortunately, the baby's sense of timing was as good as his father's, and Sam Michael Fox was born after Michael had completed filming chores on *Family Ties*.

MICHAEL J. FOX

▲ *Fox as Marty going back to the 1955 Hill Valley.*

▶ *Marty at the 'Enchantment Under the Sea' dance belting out the rock'n'roll classic 'Johnny B. Goode'.*

▼ *In Part III, Fox went back to 1885 and became a cowboy.*

'This is probably the last coming of age film I'll be able to do. I'm glad it's stretched out over the course of five years.'

MICHAEL J. FOX

A native of Vancouver, B.C., Michael began acting as a child, making his professional debut at the age of 15. Three years later, he moved to Los Angeles, and made his first film appearance in the Disney feature *Midnight Madness* (1980). He appeared in the series *Palmerstown, U.S.A.*, and guest-starred on shows such as *Lou Grant* and *Trapper John, M.D.* before landing the role for which he would win three Emmys and millions of devoted fans during the course of its seven season run – that of Alex P. Keaton on *Family Ties*.

If *Family Ties* made Michael a household name, *Back to the Future* made him a star. His preparation for the role came years earlier, before he ever stepped in front of a camera. 'All I did in high school was skateboard, chase girls and play in bands.' Fox also dreamed of being a rock star, and has a particular fondness for the band scenes in the film. 'After the first film came out, every time I went into a bar, they'd call me on stage to play "Johnny B. Goode". I received a gold record, which I hang with pride, even though I had absolutely nothing to do with it' (Michael lip-synched the song, sung by Mark Campbell, from a pre-recorded playback.

Fox enjoyed his role as 'tour guide' in *Back to the Future*, but admits there were times when 'I wanted to wear the lampshade, instead of just pointing at the guy who does.' The sequels gave him that opportunity, as well as being even more physically demanding. As a result of the hoverboarding, horseback riding and fighting, Fox suffered assorted nicks, bruises, cuts and sheer exhaustion. 'What is truly amazing,' he laughs, 'is that Bob Zemeckis is tireless in his quest to find new ways to torture me.'

Throughout his career, Fox has chosen roles that have challenged, and enabled him to grow as an actor. His credits include *Light of Day* (1987), *The Secret of My Success* (1987) and *Bright Lights, Big City* (1988). Prior to *Part II*, he spent four months in the jungles of Thailand, and garnered excellent reviews for his role in *Casualties of War* (1989). After the rigours of the *Back to the Future* sequels, Fox took a well deserved vacation before starting *The Hard Way*, the story of a successful comic actor trying to break out of the mould and do a gritty, dramatic film. Smiling, he asks: 'Does it sound kind of autobiographical?'

SPECIAL EFFECTS

VISTA GLIDE

'A system only limited by the human imagination'

KEN RALSTON visual effects supervisor

- *The Vista Glide is a motion-control system, created by Industrial Light and Magic (ILM), which uses a modified VistaVision camera.*
- *The focusing, dollying, panning and tilting of the camera are computer-controlled (using a software program designed by Bill Tondreau) so that the movements of the camera can be exactly duplicated take after take.*
- *It allows the same actor to play several different roles in the same scene and seemingly interact with himself.*

During the filming of *Who Framed Roger Rabbit?* Bob Zemeckis utilized a special computer-operated camera that enabled the director to mesh his live actors with animated characters. Although it was effective, the camera was limited in its movement and flexibility. Thinking ahead to his next project, Zemeckis asked if ILM could modify the system so it could perform as well as an ordinary camera. They came back to him with the Vista Glide.

'Usually,' explains Zemeckis, 'when you see a movie where the same person plays two characters in the same frame, the camera is locked down, and there's a door jamb, or some kind of straight vertical line between them, where they put the film split. Today's audiences are so sophisticated, they can see through that trick.' With the Vista Glide, Zemeckis was able to move that split back and forth within the scene, enabling actors to walk around themselves, or even pass objects between themselves.

▼ **C SIDE**
Michael changes to Marty Jr. He is able to act and react to the other characters with the aid of a miniature earpiece that plays the recorded dialogue, as well as the director's cues from previous takes.

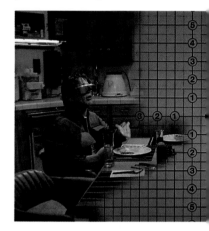

'The most difficult aspect of the Vista Glide,' says Bob Zemeckis, 'is to create a flowing performance with these different characters, when you're forced to film it in separate pieces.'

As a reference point for the start of the Vista Glide movement, a cross is pinned on the wall. The central cross-hairs of the camera must align themselves to this cross, referred to by technicians as 'home.' In the McFly farmhouse of 1885, Dean Cundey suggested the cross be affixed over the fireplace because 'home is where the hearth is . . .'

▶ *Another scene from Part II that used the Vista Glide system. Here Old Biff tries to persuade his 1955 self to take the Sporting Almanac that will make him a rich man and distort time into the 'Biffhorrific' version of 1985.*

▼ A SIDE
Shot by the camera operator in the normal method. Camera movements are recorded by the computer, which are repeated exactly when the other pieces are filmed.

'I love technical challenges,' says Michael J. Fox. 'Like when the cameraman asks me to lean a little to the left, and the sound man says "speak up", and they tell me to keep my head in the light, in addition to whatever Bob needs for the scene. Take all of that, and add the limitations of Vista Glide, and it's insanity. Trying to shoot all of the sides of the scene in the same day gave me an idea of what being in vaudeville must have been like.'

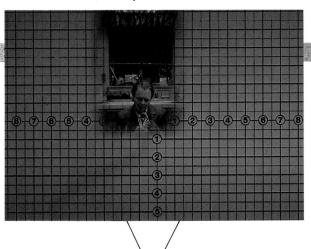

▼ B SIDE
Michael plays Marlene. Lea Thompson as Lorraine is added to the equation.

The most intricate application of the Vista Glide was the scene where Martys Sr. and Jr., and Marlene (all played by Michael J. Fox), share a pizza diner.

◄ FINISHED SHOT
After all the sides are filmed, the footage goes to ILM, where by the use of mattes and rotoscoping (hand drawing the matte around a specific feature, like an arm), the three shots are optically merged into a single image. During the filming, the director watches the action through a video monitor, connected to both the camera and computer, and can see an approximation of what the finished shot will look like.

INDUSTRIAL LIGHT AND MAGIC

- Industrial Light and Magic is a company specializing in visual effects.
- The company was founded by George Lucas in 1975 for work on Star Wars (1977), and has since produced numerous award-winning special and optical effects for countless major Hollywood productions.
- Their techniques are on the cutting edge of the industry, and their permanent staff of nearly 300 employees constantly revise and research new ideas and methods.
- ILM produced over $10 million of special effects for the Back to the Future trilogy, utilizing optical, animation and model processes needed to make cars fly, hoverboards hover and lightning strike clocktowers, among many others.

Scenes that involve special effects are filmed in VistaVision, a system developed, and abandoned, in the '50s and resurrected for special effects films such as *Star Wars* and *Raiders of the Lost Ark* (1981). The special cameras were found gathering dust by Lucas's people in a warehouse at Paramount Pictures. VistaVision is an ideal medium for special effects, as the film boasts a larger negative area than standard 35mm film. This allows a greater tolerance for the retention of optical work. After the effects are added, the film is reduced to 35mm and the image retains its clarity.

BLUE SCREEN

Some scenes require two pieces of action filmed separately, and then combined optically. The action involving the actors is filmed under controlled studio conditions, shooting against a blue background. The background upon which they will ultimately appear is shot later, using a blue filter. When the two halves are optically combined, the actors can be made to appear as if they are anywhere in this, or any other, world.

'The people at ILM are truly inspired and gifted. The first time I saw Part II, I was blown away by the flying cars, the signs on the skyway, and especially the little things like reflections of light in the cars that you wouldn't miss even if they weren't there. Their painstaking artistry adds so much to the film.'

MICHAEL J. FOX

FLYING A HOVERBOARD

In the year 2015, Marty discovers a version of a skateboard which hovers above the ground. Just as he used his makeshift skateboard in 1955 to escape from Biff, Marty uses its futuristic counterpart to foil the plans of Griff and his gang, who chase him on their larger, menacing, spiked hoverboards.

◀ *A panicked Marty is about to discover that he is not holding a normal skateboard.*

▼ *Griff's gang prepare to chase Marty on their own versions of the hoverboard.*

The hoverboard chase was filmed using a variety of techniques, and no two consecutive pieces of the chase were filmed in the same way.

Take one – The hoverboard is attached to wires, and the rider stands on the board. Although the board's movement actually propels the rider, the resulting film gives the opposite appearance.

Take two – The rider is fitted with a harness that is attached to wires, and the hoverboard is either nailed or glued to the rider's feet.

Take three – The harness was attached to a special rig suspended from a crane. This rig was equipped with steering wheels, and for each rider on a hoverboard below, a separate special effects technician was strapped on the top of the rig, suspended 100ft (30m) in the air. In the segments of the chase where we see Griff and his gang chasing Marty, a total of eight people were suspended from the crane (four on the boards, four on the rig). As the crane swung the gang into action, the technicians utilized the steering wheels to control their direction.

Take four – For some of the close-ups, rare-earth magnets, capable of attracting 600lb (272kg), were built into the futuristic Nikes, as well as the boards. As the rider is swung over the board, the magnets would snap the board up and lock it on to his feet.

Take five – When Marty is pulled along on the hoverboard by a jeep, a unique idea allowed the shot to begin on his hands (which were free) then go to his feet (on the board, which was hovering). The camera started in the air, at which point Michael J. Fox (with his Nikes screwed on to the hoverboard) is being pulled by a dolly attached to the jeep. As the camera panned down, a trapeze swung in above the camera frame. While Michael grasped the trapeze, the dolly was moved out of the way, and Marty appears to be 'hover-skiing', with assistance from the jeep.

A combination of rotoscoping and computer graphics was used by ILM to remove any traces of the wires in post-production.

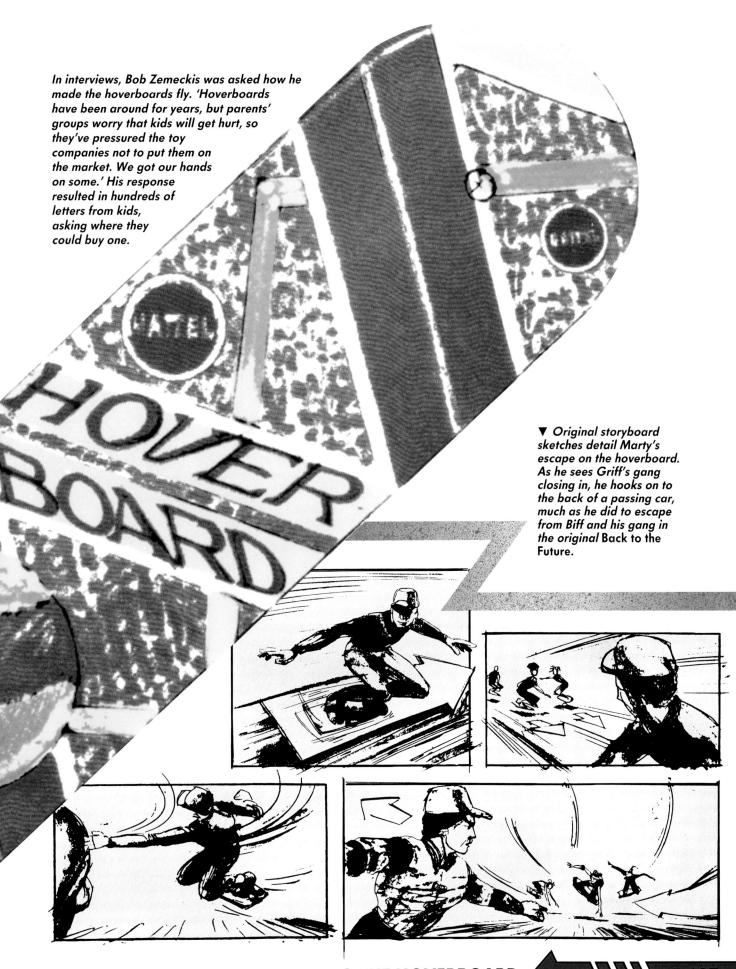

In interviews, Bob Zemeckis was asked how he made the hoverboards fly. 'Hoverboards have been around for years, but parents' groups worry that kids will get hurt, so they've pressured the toy companies not to put them on the market. We got our hands on some.' His response resulted in hundreds of letters from kids, asking where they could buy one.

▼ Original storyboard sketches detail Marty's escape on the hoverboard. As he sees Griff's gang closing in, he hooks on to the back of a passing car, much as he did to escape from Biff and his gang in the original Back to the Future.

FLYING THE HOVERBOARD

THE McFLY FAMILY

T HE McFLY family is your typical American family. Sometimes. Actually, it depends on what year you find them in, and in which version of the space-time continuum. Overall, if you were taking the census, the McFlys, at various moments throughout the Back to the Future trilogy, would fit into almost every social class and economic category.

LEA THOMPSON

LORRAINE

▼ 'Of the comedy roles I've done, young Lorraine is my favourite,' says Lea. 'She's very stylized, as a result of Bob's direction. It's a classic character – a sexy, innocent thing. She reminded me of a cat in heat.'

'My agent told me that in the movies women either play virgins, whores or mothers. The great thing about Back to the Future *is that I get to play all three.'*

LEA THOMPSON

Lea Thompson is a bright, vivacious woman, an actress who has starred with some of the most popular actors of this generation, from Tom Cruise in *All the Right Moves* (1983) to Michael J. Fox.

A native of Minneapolis, Thompson moved to New York at the age of 19 after a stint in professional ballet and modern dance, to pursue a career as an actress. She was cast in a series of commercials, which led to a small role in her first feature, *Jaws 3-D* (1983). '3-D is a very difficult technical process,' recalls Lea. 'I had no idea at the time, that my first movie was merely an introduction into the technological world of filmmaking I would be thrust into.' She came to the attention of Robert Zemeckis while he was watching *The Wild Life* (1984), starring Eric Stoltz, the original Marty. 'Bob liked me, and I got lucky.' and Thompson was awarded her first major screen role. She, like all of the cast members, had a challenging task right from the start. Her first experience as Lorraine saw her in three different versions of the character. In the second film, she again plays three Lorraines, and in *Part III*, Thompson reprises the 47-year-old Lorraine, and introduces the part of Maggie McFly in 1885.

'In the confines of a series of films that move so quickly, I tried to create characters that would make an impact, despite the velocity at which they go by. It would be easy not to worry about the little nuances of acting in this kind of situation, but

Bob Zemeckis keeps us honest.'

After *Back to the Future*, Lea worked continuously for a year and a half on films such as *Space Camp* (1986) and *Howard the Duck* (1986), having little time to revel in the success that *Back to the Future* afforded her. She has a vivid memory of watching the film for the first time in a theatre, and her delight in hearing the laughter of the audience throughout the entire movie.

MAGGIE McFLY

◀ 'Maggie comes from good Irish stock. I visited Ireland last year [1989], and I'm of Irish ancestry. I saw a bit of righteous indignation in the character, which reminded me of my grandmother. The clothing also plays an important role in establishing a base for the character. Wearing a corset, for instance, makes you sit up higher, creating a more formal attitude. What makes Maggie extra special for me is that she's my first Back to the Future character that isn't just another incarnation of Lorraine.'

LORRAINE McFLY Aged 47

◀ Lea found that the 3½-hour make-up sessions required for her transformation helped to prepare the character. 'When getting into costume and make-up, you slowly start psyching yourself into the role. Since this was a gradual process, watching it go on piece by piece, I became more and more part of the character, and the psychological change into Lorraine at 47 just happened.'

LORRAINE McFLY Aged 77

◀ 'What's remarkable about the process is that even though my face was totally covered with prosthetics, it was still me. The make-up does put the extra years on, but one can still see the person underneath, almost to the point of being able to see the passage of time that leads to what you're seeing on the screen.'

LORRAINE BAINES McFLY TANNEN

▼ 'I'm at the point in my career,' says Lea, 'where people think of me as merely an ingénue. As one grows as an actress, you get excited at the prospects of playing "diva" roles like Lorraine in Part II. One of the things that I loved about her was that she's so different from me. I wanted to portray her as a victim, yet one who hasn't been broken. She has kept a measure of integrity, sacrificing herself for the welfare of her family. It gave me the chance to play a classic female role – the martyr. It was also fun to play my first drunk scene in a movie, and what better motivation can you have for playing someone who's drunk than being married to a guy like Biff Tannen?'

For Lea, the sequels proved even more technically challenging than *Part I*. 'It's hard to remember you're an actor, and not just a prop that has to hit certain marks. The acting has to stay alive while considering technical limitations. The hardest thing is the waiting. I love to act, and on these films, I sometimes get .the feeling that I'm paid to wait around, and do the acting for free.'

▲ George McFly (Crispin Glover), Marty's father to be, keeps an eye on his loved one, Lorraine.

CRISPIN GLOVER
GEORGE McFLY

in *Part I*, Crispin Glover had a challenging role: he had to play three versions of George McFly — first as a shy, insecure teenager of 17, as well as two versions of the character at 47, one a loser, the other a successful author. Glover was no stranger to teenage screen roles. He played a rebellious teenager in *Teachers*, and also appeared in *Racing With the Moon*, and *My Tutor*. He has guest starred in TV shows such as *Happy Days*, *Hill Street Blues*, and *Family Ties*. Glover was one of the few actors who chose not to return for the sequels. His part was taken over by Jeffrey Weissman, an actor found by the producers in their very own backyard — Weissman performed impressions of Stan Laurel and Charlie Chaplin on the Universal Studios tour.

CLAUDIA WELLS/ELISABETH SHUE
JENNIFER

▼ Jennifer has the shock of her life as she meets her 2015 self, now married to Marty and mother of two children, in the McFly house.

Claudia Wells, who plays Marty's girlfriend Jennifer in *Part I*, studied opera and dance before turning to acting. She has made appearances in such television series as *Family*, *Simon and Simon*, *Trapper John, M.D.* and *Fame*, and co-starred in the series *Off the Rack*. When the cast was reassembled for the *Back to the Future* sequels, Wells was not available. The part of Jennifer was turned over to Elisabeth Shue. In *Part II*, Shue was not only required to play the 17-year-old Jennifer, but her 47-year-old future self as well. The actress was seen as Ralph Macchio's girlfriend in *The Karate Kid*, and starred in *Adventures In Babysitting*. She also starred opposite Tom Cruise in the 1988 hit *Cocktail*.

CHANGING AGES

'An actor needs patience, concentration and endurance in full rubber make-up.'

MICHAEL MILLS, make-up artist

BACKGROUND

In the original *Back to the Future*, Bob Zemeckis decided that the same actors would play their characters at different ages, a decision that carried through to the sequels as well. As the majority of the principal cast were young actors, the problem arose of how to age them from 17 to 77. Make-up artist Ken Chase ran a series of tests for the first film but the initial results were less than satisfactory. Crispin Glover, who played George McFly in *Part I*, was given a complete facelift, using a total skullcap with a receding hairline. The effect was deemed too drastic and the more subtle approach of adding prosthetic pieces to the actors' faces was hit upon. Chase designed the style for the first film, with Michael Mills, Kenny Myers and Bron Roylance taking over for the remainder of the trilogy.

The application of the make-up created many problems for the actors. Since it takes an average of three to four hours to complete, it was necessary for them to arrive at the studio at 3 am each day. The appliances would get quite hot throughout the course of the shooting day, especially for Tom Wilson and Lea Thompson who had both head and neck covered as Old Biff and

▲ *Lorraine, George and Marlene, showing how far the make-up artist's art has progressed.*

Lorraine. The rubber also makes it difficult for the skin to breathe and the actors are not able to scratch or adjust the make-up. No less an inconvenience was the necessity for the actors to exaggerate their facial movements through the layers of make-up. In order to adjust their acting techniques, hours were spent rehearsing in front of mirrors before exposing themselves to the scrutiny of the camera.

THE PROCESS

• A head-cast is taken of the actor's face and a mould is made. This mould is broken up into smaller sections such as cheeks, ears and nose.
• A sculpture of the actor's face at the desired age is created. After Bob Zemeckis has approved the sculpture, it is cut up and more casts are moulded and blended into the required shapes.

• Foam latex pieces are produced, which are glued to the actor's skin. Pancake make-up is used to blend the thin edges of the rubber appliances with the skin of the actor, so that the camera cannot detect the seam.
• Hair, in the form of sideburns, eyebrows and wigs, is added to the base.
• For the extremes of old age, liver spots are painted on the hands, while a rubber-based moulding compound is also applied. As the compound dries, it shrinks, giving hands a wrinkled effect.
• With the addition of proper lighting, the young actors appear as their older counterparts.

'When you're disguised under all that make-up,' says Lea Thompson, 'the job of acting becomes both easier psychologically and harder physically. Before I step in front of the camera, it's important that I can see the illusion that I'm trying to create. This kind of extreme make-up helps that process. Part of the actors' job is to make themselves believe they're another character, before they can expect an audience to accept them.'

The actor who undoubtedly went through the most arduous make-up schedule was Thomas F. Wilson. 'It was quite a difficult experience,' he says of the ageing process. 'I tried to downplay the physical discomfort and concentrate on how it benefited the character, but there's no denying that it's the most difficult thing I've ever done. Your skin goes crazy from the chemicals, which burn during the application and removal. It's also a claustrophobic experience, being encased in very constricting rubber and glue from my upper chest to the tip of my head, and doing it on a day-to-day basis for several weeks at a time. It was a true psychological challenge to retain enough concentration to approach the character correctly and maintain the performance.' On more than one occasion, while shooting with the Vista Glide system in *Part II*, Wilson would have to portray both Old Biff and Young Biff in the same day. The actor would begin getting into the old age make-up at 3 am, film his scenes as Old Biff, have the make-up removed and then get remade into Young Biff to act opposite himself. 'It would have been easier,' concedes Wilson, 'if we were doing *The Patty Duke Show*, and I could have just put a bow in my hair and come back as Cathy, who enjoys a minuet.'

SEAMUS McFLY

MARTY McFLY

MARTY McFLY

MARLENE McFLY　　　MARTY McFLY JR.

MAGGIE McFLY

BUFORD TANNEN

LORRAINE

BIFF TANNEN

GEORGE McFLY

LORRAINE McFLY

BIFF TANNEN

GEORGE McFLY

LORRAINE TANNEN

BIFF TANNEN

LORRAINE McFLY

BIFF TANNEN

GEORGE McFLY

GRIFF TANNEN

Michael J. Fox, the only principal cast member to have avoided the rigours of prosthetic make-up in *Part I*, found himself firmly planted in the make-up chair for the sequels, as he underwent the transformation to the 47-year-old Marty McFly, as well as Marty Jr., Marlene and Seamus. 'They put it on with airplane glue, and take it off with gasoline,' says Fox. 'It's not the most pleasant feeling in the world but from an acting standpoint, when the cameras are rolling, that's when the fun starts. Actors have been known to have some inhibitions when it comes to dealing with their own flesh, but under two inches of rubber you suddenly acquire a freedom to experiment. When the make-up is applied for the first time, you look in a mirror a lot, play with it, and see how natural it feels and looks. I know every facial expression in my repertoire, but with the addition of prosthetics, that range is suddenly extended.'

'The make-up technicians did a spectacular job,' says Bob Zemeckis, 'but one has to give the actors their due. We now have the technology to use make-up to get anyone to look like they're 47 or 77, but the actor has the power to make it live. Michael, Lea and Tom made those characters believable through their acting.'

The time range of the Back to the Future *films is evident in this 'family tree', which shows the changing ages of the main stars: (l. to r.) Michael J. Fox, Lea Thompson, Thomas F. Wilson and Crispin Glover/Jeffrey Weissman.*

THE DOC
BACKYARD GENIUS

DOCTOR EMMETT BROWN is in many ways the heart of Back to the Future, the man without whom the adventure of time travel could not take place. 'My image of Doc,' says Christopher Lloyd, 'has always been a combination of Albert Einstein and Leopold Stokowski. Doc read Jules Verne when he was 12, and was turned on by the romance of science, the excitement of discovery and the joy of creation.'

Doc Brown seeks no notoriety from his work. 'The purpose of time travel,' he explains to Marty, 'is to gain a clearer perception of humanity: where we've been, where we're going, the pitfalls and the possibilities, the perils and the promises ... perhaps even an answer to that universal question: "Why?"'

DR. EMMETT BROWN

'Doc is a Merlin figure, a magician. He's a guy who's obsessed with science and can't help but constantly invent things.'

BOB ZEMECKIS

When casting Back to the Future, everyone agreed that Christopher Lloyd was the only man for the role of Doc. Neil Canton had worked with Lloyd on The Adventures of Buckaroo Banzai, and brought him to the attention of Bob Zemeckis and Bob Gale. 'Whatever you need, Chris gives you,' says Canton. 'He's fresh and original, and while you never quite know what you're going to get with Chris, you do know it's going to be terrific.'

What very few people know is that when he was first contacted about playing the Doc, the actor seriously considered turning down the role. When the offer came, Chris was doing a film in Mexico.

'When I received the script,' he recalls, 'my first thought was that I had never been overly enthusiastic about this type of film. I also had an offer to do a play that I was very interested in. I also wasn't familiar with this Bob Zemeckis guy, so the script went into the trash can.' It was Lloyd's future wife, Carol, who convinced him that he should reconsider the project, and at least meet with the director. 'After flying to L.A. and meeting with Bob Zemeckis, Bob Gale and Neil Canton, I was ready to put on the wig and hop into the DeLorean.'

'Chris brings sort of a controlled insanity to the role of Doc Brown,' says Bob Zemeckis. 'He's able to use that ability to infuse the character with energy, without making other characters or the audience feel uncomfortable.'

On the set, Lloyd constantly astounds and amuses fellow cast and crew members with outrageous and hilarious improvisation. More than one take has been lost due to the spontaneous

'Chris Lloyd exists on a different level than you or I, but it's a wonderful level, as Chris is such a sweet man. The guy would do anything for you – he's very giving in the work process. He also exudes a gentle insanity, which greatly contributes to the chemistry between us. As an actor, I've found that you can only give a true spontaneous reaction to a situation the first time you're presented with it. When you work with Chris Lloyd, every time is the first time. You never have any idea what's going to happen. You just know it's going to be great.'

MICHAEL J. FOX

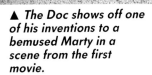

▲ The Doc shows off one of his inventions to a bemused Marty in a scene from the first movie.

▶ Marty and Jennifer are confronted by the Doc with a warning from the future.

laughter he elicits from his co-workers.

When not in front of the cameras, Lloyd rarely gives interviews or expounds upon his craft. He has earned enormous respect from the crew for his professionalism, and the ability to give each person the time they need to do their job. 'Christopher is a wonderful enigma,' says David McGiffert. 'He is anything but predictable, and every take is a wonderful surprise.'

'Chris is very quiet on the set,' adds Bob Gale, 'yet when it's time for him to act, he just turns something on, and suddenly Doc Brown is there. You wonder how much of it is conscious, or just an amazing instinct.'

But the actor works hard for his success. 'I have a vision in my mind of how I want to punctuate a scene, and if everything comes off exactly as planned, those are the most satisfying moments.' Although the actor claims several moments in the films that he would have done differently given the chance, every person on the set would agree that his performance is nothing less than inspired.

Lloyd found *Part II* the most difficult of the trilogy, as part of his function was to help the story along with lengthy tracts of exposition. While many actors would find it a Herculean task to memorize the enormous amount of dialogue that Lloyd had to deliver, the actor methodically pores over his lines, until as he puts it, 'a bomb could explode in my face, and I could keep reciting'.

DR. EMMETT BROWN ◀

CHRISTOPHER LLOYD
THE DOC

Born in Stanford, Connecticut, Christopher Lloyd knew from a very young age that he wanted to be an actor. Apprenticing in summer stock as a teenager, he moved to New York at the age of 20. He appeared in numerous off-Broadway productions, and later on Broadway in a production of *Happy End*, in which he starred opposite a then-unknown Meryl Streep.

During this time Lloyd went on countless auditions for movies but never got the parts. 'Some actors never make that transition, and I resigned myself to the fact that I was one of them.' Director Milos Forman didn't acept Lloyd's 'resignation', and he gave the actor his first screen role in *One Flew Over the Cuckoo's Nest* (1975).

Since then, Lloyd has amassed an extensive and diverse list of film credits. They include *Goin' South* (1978), *Track 29*, *Star Trek III* (1984), *The Onion Field* (1979), *Eight Men Out* and *The Dream Team*. In between *Back to the Future Part I* and *Part II*, he continued working with Bob Zemeckis in an episode of Steven Spielberg's *Amazing Stories*, and as Judge Doom in *Who Framed Roger Rabbit?* On television, Christopher has won two Emmys for his portrayal of Reverend Jim on *Taxi*.

Following the completion of *Part III*, Lloyd hopped on a plane to Cambridge, Massachusetts, for a return to the world of the theatre.

DOC'S DOGS

• *Einstein, Doc's faithful dog, is played by Freddie in* Part II *and* Part III. *Freddie is a 4½-year-old mutt, who has appeared on TV's* Dear John *and* Family Matters. *After the rigours of the filming, Freddie planned to take some time off, relax, and use part of his earnings to hire another dog to chase cars for him.*
• *The original artiste who played Copernicus, Doc's 1955 dog, was too old to return to the role he had created. The part went to Foster, a 5-year-old terrier mix. Since Foster's hair was not the same colour as the original Copernicus's, he had it dyed for the films and went back to his more natural look afterwards.*

◀ Doc's 1985 ingenuity is still at work, even in 1885. He has managed to modify his rifle with a telescopic sight that enables the weapon to 'shoot fleas off a dog at 500 yards', which gives Doc a decided edge when he arrives in the nick of time to save Marty from Buford.

▼ The Doc doesn't pay much attention to fashion, yet he is a man whose clothing constantly changes with the times. His shirts sometimes reflect things to come. In Part III, when Marty prepares to take the DeLorean from 1955 to 1885, Doc's Hawaiian shirt just happens to be emblazoned with lariats and cacti.

THE TIME MACHINE

'If you're going to build a time machine into a car, why not do it with some style?'

DR. EMMETT BROWN

'It is part of the mythology of America,' says Bob Gale, 'to say that some guy invented a reusable match or a car that gets 200 mpg, but Big Business won't let us have it. Given that premise, Bob and I figured that time travel would be invented by some crazy guy in his garage.' Adds Zemeckis, 'Doc has a believable madness about him. You believe that if he invented a time machine, it would work. The hardest thing about designing it was to give it a home-made look, as opposed to a high-tech sheen. You always had to feel the thing might explode at any minute.'

• *Emmett Brown literally 'stumbled' onto the key to time travel on 5 November 1955. Doc was standing on the toilet hanging a clock, when he fell and hit his head on the sink. When he came to, he had 'a vision, a picture in my head of the device that makes time travel possible – the flux capacitor'. Some 30 years later, the Doc unveils his latest invention – 'The one I've been waiting for my whole life.' Within the stainless steel frame of a DeLorean motor car, Doc has built a time machine. On the dashboard is a display with three digital readouts: destination time, present time and last time departed. Input your destination time, and when the car reaches a speed of 88 mph, the DeLorean shatters the time barrier, leaving a trail of flame behind.*

• *In the parking lot of the Twin Pines shopping mall, at exactly 1.19 on the morning of 26 October 1985, Doc's dream becomes reality. His dog, Einstein, becomes the world's first time traveller, going one minute into the future. Several minutes later Doc's young protégé, Marty McFly, accidentally becomes the world's second time traveller, heading 30 years into the past.*

- To send the DeLorean through time, Doc must create a nuclear reaction (utilizing plutonium stolen from terrorists) to generate the 1.21 jigowatts of electricity needed to power the flux capacitor. When Marty is stranded in the past, the 1955 Doc must find an alternative energy source, as plutonium is not readily available. Luckily Marty has some 'inside' information on the weather, and Doc channels a lightning bolt through the flux capacitor and sends the youth back to 1985.

- Returning from 2015, Doc shows Marty the new improvements in the time machine. Plutonium is no longer necessary, as the flux capacitor is powered by 'Mr. Fusion', a device that converts waste into energy. He has also fitted the car with a 'hover conversion', enabling the DeLorean to fly.

- Returning to 1955 for the second time, the DeLorean is caught in the same lightning storm that helped send Marty back to 1985 in the first place. With Doc at the wheel, a lightning bolt hits the time machine, causing a jigowatt overload which scrambles the time circuits, and sends the vehicle, and Doc, to 1885. The overload also destroys the car's flying circuits. As the technology to repair the time machine does not exist in 1885, Doc buries the car in an abandoned mine, and uses several generations of Western Union to deliver a message to Marty, along with instructions for the '55 Doc to fix the DeLorean. In a sense, it is the 1985 Doc who teaches his younger self how to build the time machine.

• *Marty travels to 1885 to rescue Doc. Upon his arrival, he inadvertently puts a hole in the gas tank. Searching for a fuel replacement, Doc tries the saloon's 180 proof whisky, which promptly blows out the fuel injection manifold. Doc and Marty hit upon the idea of pushing the DeLorean with a steam engine. To increase the locomotive's power and speed, Doc creates special logs, chemically treated to burn hotter and longer. Seconds before the car hits 88mph, Doc returns to the steam engine to save Clara, and is stranded in the past as the DeLorean disappears through time. As Marty returns to 1985, the time machine is destroyed in a crash with a diesel train. Doc is gone, and time travel is lost forever. Or is it?*

TIME TRAVEL EFFECT

The visual effect of time travel is a combination of practical, optical and animated processes. On screen, the effect lasts scant seconds, yet it is the product of months of intricate and detailed work, beginning with the filming, and finished in post-production at ILM.
• *As the car approaches 88mph, the flux capacitor (controlled off-screen by a technician) gives off a white glow.*
• *Neon coils on the side of the car emit a blue glow. This effect is later enhanced optically to give the colour a greater intensity.*
• *Animated streams of light and particles emanate from a device on the roof of the car.*
• *A pyrotechnic effect using flashbulbs provides the white flash signalling that the DeLorean has broken the time barrier.*
• *Technicians laid down two tracks of a chemical compound on the street to provide the fire trails left in the car's wake.*

Seven DeLoreans, including one 'process' car which can be dismantled for easy access, and a lightweight fibreglass model, were used in the filming. For the first movie, many of the accessories for the DeLorean were constructed from war surplus supplies. When *Part II* began production, three more cars were purchased. Unfortunately, many of the war surplus parts were no longer available, and had to be re-created by hand. The 2015 Mr. Fusion attachment was fashioned from a Krupps coffee grinder. One of them currently serves as a lamp in producer Bob Gale's office.

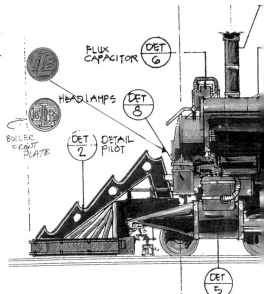

THE JULES VERNE TRAIN

As Marty and Jennifer comb through the wreckage of the decimated DeLorean, they are suddenly knocked over by a huge blast of wind. Doc Brown has returned in a new time machine, built from a steam engine. Having returned to 1985 to retrieve Einstein, Doc announces that he and Clara have been married, and introduces his sons, Jules and Verne. As Doc prepares for lift-off, Marty asks if he's planning to go back to the future. 'Nope', says the Doc. 'Already been there . . .'

Production designer Rick Carter took his inspiration for the new time machine from the submarine *Nautilus* in Disney's *20,000 Leagues Under the Sea* (1954). 'Since Doc has always been enamoured with the writings of Jules Verne, it seemed the obvious choice.'

Doc, Clara and their children then fly off on a new time-travel adventure — 'but one that I'm not going to direct', swears Bob Zemeckis.

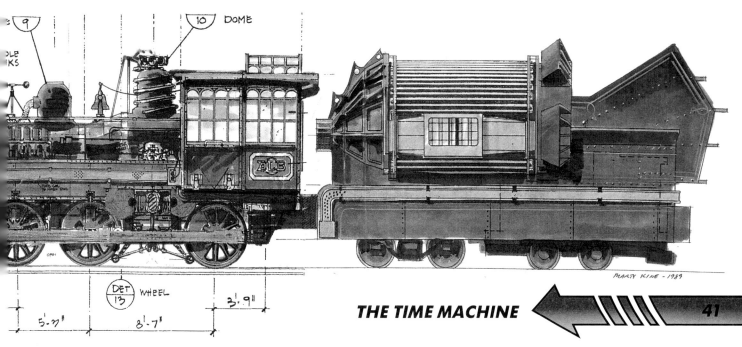

MARTY KLINE - 1989

◄ *Original storyboards illustrate the progress that has been made in transportation as Doc, Marty and Jennifer arrive in Hill Valley in the year 2015.*

FLYING CARS

'I've waited my whole life to drive around in a flying car.'

BOB GALE

The 1939 World's Fair predicted that by the end of the century, cars would fly. Bob Gale was eager to believe this prophecy, but as the years passed, he realized that if he ever hoped to see a flying car before the year 2000, he and Bob Zemeckis would have to be the ones to make it fly.

In *Back to the Future*, we get our first glimpse of a flying car, as Doc returns to take Marty and Jennifer to 2015. When they arrive there in *Part II*, flying cars are commonplace items. They soar across the skyways, and as they land, the wheels unfold and are suitable for ordinary travel on land. Like many of the other special effects in the trilogy, the flying cars are a result of the efforts of both the shooting and post-production crews.

'What makes these effects work so well,' says Bob Gale, 'is that we take them for granted. If the audience is involved in the story, the effects are there to enhance their enjoyment, and make the story more believable, not to call attention to themselves. We tried to make sure these effects were so tightly incorporated into the story, no one would question how they were done until they were on their way home from the theatre.'

FEATS OF FLIGHT

A lightweight, full-size fibreglass DeLorean was built, complete with radio-controlled wheels. This DeLorean was flown by wires with the aid of a crane. In other scenes, the car was hoisted from behind by a fork-lift.

Production designer Rick Carter's unique set design gave the filmmakers another method to simulate flight. In the alley where Doc first lands the DeLorean in 2015, there is a black gap where two walls meet. The space was filled with brushes like those found in a car wash. On the other side of the wall, a crane arm slowly lowered the time machine to the ground. As the arm descended, the brushes closed around it, effectively hiding the mechanism responsible for the car's landing.

MODELS

Several of the flying car shots were filmed using a one-fifth

◄ At Industrial Light and Magic, the model of the time machine is positioned for the camera. Inside the car are scale-sized puppets of Marty and Doc. Just as the DeLorean model is repositioned for every frame of film shot, so are the movements of the 'driver' and 'passenger' inside the car.

▼ A one-fifth scale model of the futuristic taxicab was also built, and photographed in flight. In the film, we see the cab leave Old Biff in Hilldale and fly away in a single camera shot that combines footage of the real cab with actor Tom Wilson, and this model.

scale model of the DeLorean, built by ILM under the supervision of Steve Gawley. It is an exact reproduction of the car, accurate in every detail, and comes with a puppet driver and passenger. Activated by a servo-mechanism, the model is capable of a variety of functions and has its own electronic circuitry, which supplies power to the flux capacitor, time displays, the headlights and the neon coils, among many others. The wheels are made of aluminium, because the lights inside them (simulating the car's thrust) burned too hot to make rubber a viable consideration. Three miniature fans cool the inside of the car, which can accommodate rods to hold it in five different positions, for filming various angles.

Models are specifically built according to what the camera will photograph, and many of them are only shells. In addition to the DeLorean, models were built of the police car and motorcycle, and the taxicab, as well as other futuristic prototypes. Skyway markers and lights seen in the descent into Hill Valley were also built to scale. 'The skill of making models,' says Gawley, 'is to make them totally believable. The biggest thrill is being able to make a model which is indistinguishable from the real thing.'

FILMING MODELS

On the special effects stage, a model car is programmed by computer to move in one direction, while the camera moves in another. At times, the model is stationary, and the camera does the travelling. These moves are shot at the rate of one frame per second, with the car advancing at a greatly reduced pace. When the completed image is projected at the standard 24 frames per second, the effect is one of normal movement.

A single movement can be shot as many as eight times. First comes the master shot, known as the 'beauty pass', filming the car's action against a blue background. Next come the effects passes, filming elements such as shadows from street lights. The wheel lights, headlights and interior lights are all filmed separately, and finally a pass is shot with the addition of smoke, to achieve a spotlight effect through the haze. The shots are filmed separately in order to give the director maximum flexibility in the final composite.

A FAVOURITE SHOT

In *Part II*, when Doc, Marty and Jennifer return to 1985 from the future, the audience watches the car fly down the street, land, and pull into a driveway where its occupants get out. Although it appears to be a single shot, it is in fact two, and is the ultimate merger of miniature model work and actual shooting.

As the flying miniature descends onto the street, it passes behind a street light and the real DeLorean emerges on the other side. Zemeckis first shot Chris and Michael in the car, then turned the footage over to ILM. Visual effects supervisor Ken Ralston and ILM camera operator Peter Daulton worked backwards from the live footage, to duplicate the moves of the actual DeLorean with those of its miniature counterpart. When the two pieces were optically linked, the resulting footage appears to have captured the action with a single pan. It is the first time that anyone has ever been able to successfully turn a model into the real McCoy in a single shot. 'It is a true test of the skill of the cameraman and the craftsmanship of the modelmaker,' says Gawley.

DOC'S LABORATORY

'*We wanted to establish the Doc's character before we physically introduced him. By showing these incredibly elaborate and silly inventions, we were able to set up his character, and set the tone for the film.*'
BOB ZEMECKIS

The very first moments of *Back to the Future* pan across Doc's lab to reveal an enormous collection of clocks, which tell us more than just what time it is. They are, in their varied sizes and designs, a 'calling card' of their owner, who is further identified by the revelation of a do-it-yourself breakfast-making/dog-feeding machine.

Doc is the epitome of the American ideal – the man who can invent anything in his own backyard. His inventions, including the time machine, have the look and feel of projects which are home-made, and as often as not don't work.

The '50s segments of Doc's house and lab in *Part 1* were shot in Pasadena. The exterior and interior of the impressive complex are two well-known Green & Green designs, the Gamble House and the Blacker-Hill House. The filmmakers returned to the Gamble House for *Part III*, to shoot the exterior of Doc's home, and re-created the interior on a soundstage.

Doc's inventions are an integral part of the *Back to the Future* trilogy. They are elaborate Rube Goldberg-type ventures, which help to (1) satisfy the Doc's thirst for knowledge, (2) test the skills of the people who design them for the films, and (3) provide a major source of amusement for the people watching the films.

◄ *The Doc is a man who leaves nothing to chance. In his 1955 lab he builds a scale version of the Hill Valley town square, to demonstrate how the lightning will be conducted through the DeLorean to send Marty back to 1985.*

► *Stranded in 1885, Doc builds yet another model, which details his plan of using a steam engine to push the DeLorean up to the required 88 miles per hour and return him and Marty back to the future.*

A BIT OF HOME

The Doc has happily accepted his life in 1885, but there are some 20th-century amenities he can't do without. So he applies his 1985 knowledge to the 19th-century problem and invents an enormous contraption that takes up most of his workshop. It comprises steam boilers, wind generators, leaky pipes and leather fan belts. When Doc pulls the switch, the device quakes and trembles, emitting a huge burst of smoke. After several seconds a small object drops out of the spout. Doc places the object in a beaker filled with brown liquid, which he offers to Marty. 'Iced tea?' he asks.

BREAKFAST MACHINE

In *Back to the Future* Doc had invented a machine that automatically made his breakfast and fed Einstein. In *Part III* he produces a similar device in 1885 — this one without the aid of electricity.

When the chicken lays an egg (hidden in a special compartment), it rolls down a chute into a bowl. It is cracked and transferred sunny-side up into a frying pan. The pan moves along a belt to a burner on the stove (pre-heated by the special effects department), where the egg begins to cook. Strips of bacon roll through a washing machine wringer, and a candle burns through a piece of string, which causes the toast to pop up. Breakfast is served.

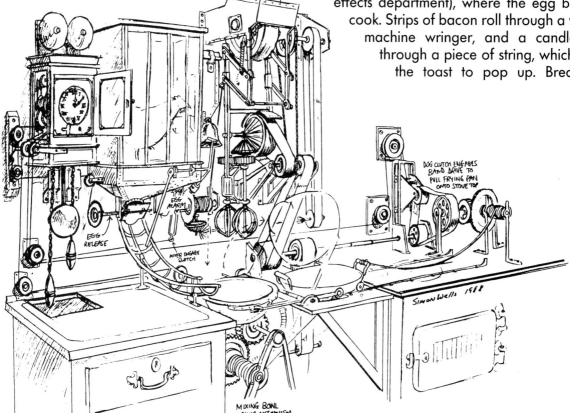

CLARA
THE SCHOOL MARM

Mary Steenburgen was the filmmakers' first and only choice to play Clara Clayton, the 1885 schoolteacher who falls in love with Doc Brown.

▼ *Clara takes off in pursuit of her beloved Emmett, hoping to catch up with the train that Doc has commandeered to send himself and Marty back to the future.*

'Clara has always been a bit of a misfit in her time,' says Mary Steenburgen of her character. 'When she meets someone who is from another time, everything becomes clear to her. She falls in love with Emmett from the very moment they meet. Theirs is an old-fashioned, romantic love story.'

While the filmmakers decided from the start that Mary was perfect for the role, the actress was equally excited about joining the *Back to the Future* family. 'I have enormous respect for Bob Z's knowledge of film, not only in a classic sense, but also of everything that's innovative. He's on the cutting edge, and also has a great bullshit detector. Even while concentrating on the innumerable technical aspects of a scene, he can spot a false note in the performance.'

Mary relished the chance to participate in what would be her second western. Her first was also her screen debut, *Goin' South*, starring Jack Nicholson (and Christopher Lloyd). 'If you've never done one,' says the actress, 'you tend to take westerns for granted, but if you know how infrequently in your career you're going to get the opportunity to be in one, you treasure those occasions.'

The actress did many of her own stunts, finding herself on a galloping horse in pursuit of a train, on top of the train with sparks and pyrotechnics surrounding her, and falling into the tender car, as the train sped along its route. She planned everything well in advance with the aid of her stunt double, Jennifer Watson, and was always aware of the parameters of those stunts. 'I did the dangerous stuff, Jennifer did the *incredibly* dangerous stuff,' Mary confides. 'It was physically arduous but I enjoyed myself, despite the measure of danger involved.' Her children, who travelled to location with Mary, visited the set on one occasion to find their mother – clad in a vivid purple dress – hanging upside-down from a train. Having been exposed to the motion picture industry for most of their lives, they took it in their stride.

◄ *Clara and Doc became further enamoured of each other as they dance the night away at the Hill Valley festival.*

MARY STEENBURGEN

CLARA

▲ *At the festival Clara watches with deep concern as Buford 'Mad Dog' Tannen prepares to shoot her new-found love, Emmett Brown.*

Raised in Little Rock, Arkansas, Mary Steenburgen relocated to New York to study acting in 1972. Five years later she chanced to meet Jack Nicholson while waiting for an audition. Nicholson was looking for a leading lady for the film he was about to direct and star in. After having had her read a scene, he sent her off to Hollywood for a screen test and the part was hers.

Ironically, the co-star of that film was Christopher Lloyd, playing a character named Towfield, whose advances are spurned by Mary in favour of Nicholson. 'Chris said the first line anybody ever said to me on screen,' recalls Mary. 'It was: "I asked you out a thousand times, and all you gave me was the plait of your umbrella." In Sonora I had a picture taken of us, and sent it to Jack with a note, saying: "It took him eighteen years, but Towfield finally gets the girl."'

Part III is Mary's first action/adventure film, but not her first time-travel film. She encountered a man from a different century in the form of H.G. Wells (portrayed by Malcolm McDowell) in *Time After Time* (1979).

Mary received an Academy Award for her role in *Melvin and Howard* (1980), and has also starred in the films *Cross Creek* (1983), *A Midsummer Night's Sex Comedy* (1982), *Ragtime* (1981), *Romantic Comedy* (1983), and most recently, opposite Steve Martin in *Parenthood* (1989).

The train sequences in *Part III* held an additional, and very special meaning for the actress. 'The train was important to me, because my father was a freight train conductor, and I was always climbing around trains with him. He passed away when I was filming *Parenthood*, and as I worked on the train in Sonora, it brought back some very special memories for me.'

◄ *Doc tells Clara the truth – he is from the year 1985 and must return to his own time. Clara doesn't believe the scientist, thinking it's his way of breaking off their relationship. She stands at the station, waiting for a train that will take her and her broken heart away from Hill Valley.*

BUFORD, BIFF, GRIFF AND THE GANG

BUFORD TANNEN

Buford 'Mad Dog' Tannen is, according to Tom Wilson, 'the original evil seed in the Tannen family. He's the epitome of a violent era, in which, we're told from history books, you could shoot a man over a trivial matter. I think Buford originated the concept of shooting a man for snoring.' Wilson loved watching westerns as a kid, but never thought he'd be 'the guy who walks into the saloon, and so terrifies the townsfolk that they clear out'. He enjoyed the intensive training he underwent to acquire the roping, quick-draw and shooting abilities necessary for the role. Now that he is skilled in those areas, Wilson is currently searching for a way to apply these talents to his everyday life, much to the chagrin of his family and friends.

◀ Hill Valley's resident outlaw.

▼ 1955 – the Tannen tradition continues.

THE MEMBERS of the Tannen family are the flies in the ointment of the McFlys' lives,' says Thomas F. Wilson, the man who has portrayed every one of them. From 1885 to 2015, Seamus, George, Marty and Marty Jr. have been tormented, harassed and endangered by Buford, Biff and Griff. Invariably, in the course of the Back to the Future trilogy, good triumphs over evil and the Tannens are eventually thwarted by the McFlys, prompting one crew member to observe, 'Into each McFly's life, a Tannen must fall . . .'.

▼ The alternate Biff prepares to kill Marty.

▼ Biff checks with George to see if anybody's home.

▶ Putting on the second coat.

BIFF TANNEN

Unfortunately Buford was not the last of the Tannens, and his great-grandson Biff takes over the mantle of Hill Valley town bully, a title he embraces with relish. Over the generations, Buford's traits have survived and resurfaced in Biff. While his great-grandfather threatened, 'I'll hunt you and shoot you down like a duck,' Biff displays the Tannen knack for mangling metaphors by telling people to 'make like a tree, and get out of here'.

The two Tannens also have a hobby in common – they like to intimidate people named McFly. Buford had his fun at the expense of Seamus McFly in the late 1800s, and in 1955 Biff has found his perfect victim in the shy, retiring George McFly. Tannen delights in torturing the youngster, forcing him to do Biff's homework, among other things. Whenever George doesn't respond quickly enough, he gets a rap on the head from Biff, along with the inquiry, 'Hello? Anybody home?' The object of Biff's affections is the lovely Lorraine Baines, who, in turn, wants nothing to do with him.

Over the next 30 years, Biff has continued to harass George and lust after Lorraine. In 1985, he is George's supervisor, and true to form, makes George do all the work and takes all the credit. Fortunately for George and Lorraine, their youngest son is accidentally transported to the past, where he stands up to Biff and forces his father to do so as well. In the aftermath of Marty's visit to 1955, Biff has been put in his place and now works for George. 'Biff leads an incredibly frustrating life,' says Tom Wilson. 'He just can't win,' no matter what happens, and he never gets the girl. The music just doesn't swell when he's on screen.'

BIFFHORRIFIC BIFF

Owing to Old Biff's theft of the time machine in 2015, a new, alternate version of Biff results – Biff Tannen, the 'luckiest man on earth'. Young Biff's 'luck' comes in the form of a gift from his future self – an almanac containing all the sports statistics from the years 1950–2000. It allows Biff to successfully wager on any event and amass a fortune.

Biff's new-found money and power have enabled him to turn Hill Valley into 'Hell' Valley. The town square's landmark courthouse has been transformed into Biff Tannen's Pleasure Paradise Casino and the Biff Tannen museum (where smoking is required). He owns the police force and is able to live out all his fantasies, which include killing George McFly and marrying Lorraine. Realizing his dream, Biff turns Lorraine into his version of the ideal woman – a glitzy harlot, complete with some new, over-developed, 'attributes'.

'The town under this Biff's control,' notes Tom Wilson, 'is a celebration of filth, pornography and evil. I think the key to Biff's true personality is displayed in the décor of the penthouse of his casino. Anything of artistic expression at all is on black velvet . . .'

◀ Doc warns Marty: 'Watch yourself around that Griff character. He's got a few short-circuits in his bionic implants.'

◀ Inset (top to bottom): Biff's 1955 gang: Griff and his punks prepare to deal with Marty; and Buford with his band of ruffians.

OLD BIFF

'In the future, the 78-year-old Biff is bitter about the way his life has turned out, and he blames everyone else for it,' says Wilson. 'At the end of the first movie, he seemingly changed his ways, and was no longer a threat to the McFly family. In Part II, when he discovers the existence of the time machine, he slips right back into being a sinister character, trying to turn this new discovery to his advantage.' Wilson underwent four hours of prosthetic make-up each day for Old Biff. 'In playing the character,' he notes, 'I tried to avoid becoming a caricature. It's easy to shuffle around, hunch your shoulders and use a gravelly voice, but to be able to take a slight edge off of that, and make him a real character, instead of being a young guy playing an old man, was a true challenge.'

GRIFF

In Part II, Marty and Doc Brown find that the future holds many surprises: technology has made life easier, with people having more time to enjoy simple pleasures. But as it has been noted many times, the more things change, the more they stay the same. In the year 2015, Hill Valley still has a town bully, and he's still a Tannen, better known as Griff. What's more, he still has a McFly to pick on, this one being Marty's son. It is Marty Junior's involvement with Griff that

▶ Even in the year 2015, the 78-year-old Biff continues to torment Marty, checking to see if 'anybody's home'.

brings Doc and Marty to the future to prevent a potential disaster.

The one major difference between Griff and his notorious predecessors is that he has allowed a female into his gang of three. 'Maybe Griff has come to understand that women are not necessarily inferior beings, and in regard to the qualities that he looks for in a gang member, a woman has the ability to perform the job as well as any man,' offers Wilson. 'Or maybe he let her in because he thinks she's a great-looking babe.

'Much like his grandfather, Griff has his own problems relating to the rest of society,' says Tom. 'Griff is the result of steroids, electroshock therapy and a failed lobotomy. He's just not firing on all pistons.'

THOMAS F. WILSON

BUFORD BIFF GRIFF

The eldest of five children, Tom Wilson was heavily involved in the dramatic arts in high school, as well as serving as the president of the debate team. He studied international politics at Arizona State University before turning his attention to the performing arts.

He returned home to Philadelphia, and on a whim, began performing stand-up comedy at 'open-mike' nights in the area. Polishing his act (and the tuba that he plays in it), Wilson worked his way up to comedy clubs in Baltimore, Washington, D.C. and New York. While working the clubs, he also studied acting at the American Academy of Dramatic Arts.

Wilson relocated to Los Angeles in 1981, where he found work at comedy clubs such as The Comedy Store, and the Improvisation, often doubling as the clubs' bouncer. After a number of commercials and appearances in television shows such as Knight Rider and The Facts of Life, Tom won his first big screen role — Biff in Back to the Future.

Since then, he has starred in the features April Fool's Day (1986), Let's Get Harry (1986) and Action Jackson (1988). When time permits, he continues to perform stand-up comedy. Tom Wilson has made his mark in the motion picture industry by playing a family of characters who are, in his own words, 'genetic waste'. Yet he takes it all in his stride. 'It has always been a dream of mine,' he explains, 'to be universally despised by the world's moviegoing public.'

THE CHANGING FACE OF HILL VALLEY

▲ In 1885 Marty and Doc pose in front of the same clock that will enable the '55 Doc to send Marty back to the future.

SETTING EACH PART of the trilogy in the same fictional town, Bob Zemeckis and Bob Gale gave Hill Valley, California, as much of an identity as any of the human characters in the Back to the Future films. As Doc and Marty traverse the space-time continuum, they observe the impact that time, and their actions, have had on their town.

▼ On 12 November 1955 a bolt of lightning hits the clock-tower of the Hill Valley courthouse, freezing the clock-face at 10.04.

▲ In the year 2015 the town square has undergone a rebirth as a result of the more environmentally-conscious society. The clock remains frozen at 10.04.

1885

The western has a special place in cinematic history. It depicts an era of discovery and the growth of a people in search of a dream.

▼ The set designers gave Bob Gale a place in 1885 Hill Valley history, making him editor of the local newspaper.

▼ Director of photography Dean Cundey decided to dress in the style of the period he was shooting. No one knows why.

In the late 1800s, Marty is forced to come to terms with his overly sensitive pride and bravado. In the more 'civilized' society of the 1980s, he might be able to get by with no more than a few scrapes and bruises from extraneous scuffling, but in 1885, where 'a man's gotta do what a man's gotta do', a needless confrontation has been the cause of many an unmarked grave in Boot Hill. In a violent period of American history, Marty must learn that fighting is not always the answer.

▼ Bob Zemeckis decided to cast several legends of the western film. Dub Taylor, Matt Clark, Harry Carey, Jr. and Pat Buttram (l. to r.) appear as the bartender and regular patrons of the Hill Valley saloon.

CREATING A WESTERN

In a behind-the-scenes documentary about the making of *Back to the Future Part I*, Michael J. Fox was asked where he would go if he could actually travel through time. His response? 'The old west.' After five months of production on *Part II*, he got his wish, as the cast and crew began the enormous challenge of filming the epic western.

'I grew up watching westerns,' says Bob Zemeckis, 'and while I'd never directed one, I had an instinct for it, based on the knowledge I had soaked up over the years.' Zemeckis recognizes that setting his film in the old west has its risks, as the western has suffered in popularity over the past 20 years. 'Our advantage is that, despite its setting, *Part III* is a film about time travel. We're taking a 1980s kid and sticking him in the 1880s, giving a new dimension to the western genre. We hope that our film will combine the ingredients of what people love about both westerns and the *Back to the Future* movies.'

Production designer Rick Carter set out to create a town that was still in its infancy, but would continue to grow to become the Hill Valley that audiences have become familiar with. The filmmakers decided against using the Universal Studios town square, the site of Hill Valley in *Part I* and *Part II*. 'The problem with trying to re-create the old west at a studio is that if the camera moves just a little too far in one direction, you're suddenly in 1930s New York or you run into King Kong,' says producer Neil Canton. 'We needed some elbow room.'

Carter envisioned the 1885 Hill Valley as having already been around for 30 or 40 years, and his design reflects that vision. As one heads into town from the train depot, you find the Chinese camp and shanty town, where the newcomers to the area reside. Along the main street are the first signs of commerce in the area, businesses that deal in provisions and other necessities. Finally there is the town square, with its saloon (on the site of the '50s cafe and Cafe '80s) and courthouse, as well as other future landmarks, still under construction. The square is a symbol that Hill Valley is not merely a town that sprang up to capitalize on the Gold Rush, and will soon disappear. It is a town that is going to have a history.

◀ Artist's impression of Hill Valley in 1885, with the Town Hall under construction.

WESTERN CLOTHES

Having designed the clothes for the residents of Hill Valley in the year 2015, costume designer Joanna Johnston found her task somewhat easier when it came to their 1885 ancestors. 'I had no frame of reference for the costumes of the future, but for *Part III* I was dealing with a time period I had experience with, on the movie *Tess.*' As per instructions from Bob Zemeckis, Johnston sought to make the clothes realistic to the period, and in addition to the principal cast, would have to clothe as many as 500 extras. Johnston scoured the costume houses of Hollywood, and found that most of their costumes were made for the westerns

THE COLOUR PURPLE

As Clara Clayton, Mary Steenburgen is dressed in vibrant lilac, pink and purple dresses. The purple dress, in particular, caused several problems in preproduction. Several fabrics were dyed and camera tests were shot to make sure the colour was right for the screen. The first sample proved to contain too much blue, which would hinder the optical blue-screen process. Another faded when exposed to constant sunlight. Joanna Johnston took great pains to make sure that all the extras blended into the background, but wanted Mary to 'jump off the screen, and look like a true heroine.' While Joanna may have taken a few liberties with the colours, she says that Mary's dresses were true to the period.

of the '40s, '50s and '60s, and didn't reflect the authenticity she sought. Extensive research uncovered original clothing patterns, and hundreds of new 'antique' costumes were created. The serape that Michael J. Fox wears was reproduced from an actual article of clothing from the late 1800s. Johnston used muted, earthy tones for the costumes, as she wanted the people of the town to look 'as if they were covered with dust', and had a soil sample sent from the location to get a better idea of how the materials would photograph against the red earth. 'I wanted everyone to blend into one image,' says Johnston. The natural elements of Sonora helped her achieve her goal, as by the end of each day everyone (crew members included) was coated in red dust.

▼ *The Doc's coat and Marty's serape were designed from original clothing patterns from the late 1880s.*

ON LOCATION

The cast and crew spent three and a half months in Sonora and Jamestown, California, situated in the middle of gold country. The area has served as a location for countless westerns dating back to the silent era, films ranging from *High Noon* to *Pale Rider*. Covering several acres, the *Part III* set was the largest ever constructed in the area. Accustomed to film production, the population of Sonora made the *Back to the Future* crew welcome, and many worked as extras and wranglers.

As filming progressed, assorted recreational activities sprung up around the enormous set during breaks. A volleyball court was erected, and skeetshooting and horseshoes often took the place of lunch. Michael J. Fox found a nearby pond stocked with bass and trout, and led more than one fishing expedition. After a time the set earned the nickname of 'Club Hill Valley'.

A HORSE OPERA

After hiring hundreds of extras to populate Hill Valley, the filmmakers still needed one element to complete the town – horses.

Veteran horse-trainer Corky Randall, whose father had trained horses for Roy Rogers, arranged for the transportation, care and feeding of over 90 horses on the location. In addition, it was Randall who saw to it that the horses could perform a specific action in a scene. Many of the horses were used to pull carriages or walk leisurely through the town, but the actors needed several horses each to perform a variety of duties, such as galloping, rearing, bucking or standing still. For Tom Wilson, who had grown up in Philadelphia and 'rode the subway much more than horses', the experience was an interesting one. Wilson and the rest of the cast took riding lessons on Corky's ranch and learned the intricacies of handling a horse. 'I'd ridden a horse before,' says Wilson, 'but these were real, cowboy-type horses. When you get on them, they look at you and say "Well, what do you want me to do? I'm not one of those trail guys, who walks the same path every day of my life. You gotta tell me what you want."'

In finding a large number of horses for the production, Randall had the difficult task of finding animals that were adaptable for motion picture work. Some are spooked by the sound of the machinery, and others are simply not capable of repeating the same action over and over. On *Part III*, Randall was proud to report that his horses 'came through like champions'.

Many of the wranglers were from old-time Hollywood and had worked on some of the classic westerns, but the majority of the *Back to the Future* crew was largely a young group and had to adapt their knowledge of production to accommodate some new factors. Horses pulling carriages, for instance, can't simply be backed up after the director has called 'Cut'. To reset the scene, they had to follow a circuitous route to their original positions for another take, adding several unscheduled minutes to the precious shooting time. The crew also found that horses kick up a tremendous amount of dust while manoeuvring, and after a few days of returning to their hotels caked with dirt, learned to stand upwind of the animals while they were working.

▲ *Marty is given a personally guided 'tour' of Hill Valley town square in 1885, courtesy of Buford 'Mad Dog' Tannen. The rope was not released until all of the action had come to a full stop, and experienced horsemen doubled for Buford and the gang members, and rode the horses behind the action to make sure that if the rope dragging Michael J. Fox or his stunt double had accidentally gotten loose, neither would have run the risk of being trampled on by the animals.*

▲▼ *Having already faced the threat of Indians upon his arrival in 1885 (left), Marty hides the DeLorean and watches the cavalry take off in pursuit of the tribe (below). First and second units filmed these and other scenes in Monument Valley, a location whose majestic vistas have been previously immortalized on film in legendary westerns such as* Stagecoach *and* She Wore a Yellow Ribbon.

1955

'What happened in the 1950s that has made it so nostalgic throughout the subsequent decades was that the '50s saw the "birth" of the American teenager. It was the first time that teenagers began to rule, and they've been ruling ever since.'

BOB ZEMECKIS

For the *Back to the Future* trilogy, the filmmakers had to create 1955 not once, but three times. It is the central setting of Marty's first adventure, when he meets his parents as teenagers, and in the second film he returns to the very same time, trying to retrieve the Sports Almanac from Biff as well as avoiding his other 'self'. The year 1955 is also the point of departure for Marty as he travels to 1885 to save Doc Brown in *Part III*.

On the original *Back to the Future*, the challenge was to create a town that could look quaint and fresh in 1955, but also display the passage of time and suburban expansion in 1985. Deciding it would be too difficult to use an actual town, the filmmakers built the town square on Universal's back lot. The '50s scenes were shot first and then the town was 'trashed down' to reflect the ravages of time over the ensuing 30 years.

When first designing the 1955 town square, *Back to the Future* production designer Larry Paull 'began to delve into a lot of *Life* and *Look* magazines, and used a lot of photographic research of the time. I did a lot of digging, even in old high school yearbooks, in order to come up with a feeling and a visual concept.' Paull constructed a set that featured a grassy town square surrounded by picturesque shops, which included a record store, travel agency and a malt shop painted in a vivid 1950s turquoise blue. Periods cars were brought in, primarily from the late '40s and early '50s, and the lack of foreign cars (proper for the period) is evident. 'The amount

of detail that went into that set,' recalls Michael J. Fox, 'was incredible. In the shots where I walk through the square for the first time in 1955, I had to convey a sense of amazement. On a set like that, I didn't have to act.'

In many ways, *Back to the Future*'s 1955 is not a real depiction of the era. It is one as seen through nostalgic eyes – a cleaner, fresh-faced version of the time. It is a year re-created by adults who tend to forget the negative aspects and recall things on a simple, more positive level, which is exactly the

▶ In Part II Biff continues to harass Lorraine. Tom Wilson, Lea Thompson and Lisa Freeman (as Lorraine's friend Babs) all returned to their roles, as well as the year 1955, for Part II.

▶ Mr. Strickland, the tough schoolteacher of Hill Valley High, remonstrates with Marty in the school's corridor.

sense that Zemeckis and Gale wished to convey. Their 1955 Hill Valley is a town in its heyday. Everything is new and pristine, even the local high school (shot at Whittier High School, where ex-President Richard Nixon was a student). It is the 1950s as seen with 1980s hindsight.

Four years after their original sojourn to 1955, Bob Zemeckis set the DeLorean's controls for 12 November 1955, and took his cast and crew back to the '50s for a second visit. 'That was one of the reasons I was so excited about doing the sequel,' explains Zemeckis. 'I wasn't interested in just getting the cast together, having them go on

◄ In 1955 Marty 'invents' a skateboard to escape from Biff.

▼ With Biff and his gang closing in behind, Marty gets a lift from a truck.

another adventure, and call it the sequel to *Back to the Future*. Since we accept the fact that Doc Brown has invented a viable method of time travel, we were able to do something that had never been done in a sequel before – to go back into the first movie and rewitness scenes from that film from a completely different perspective. We deliberately designed scenes to jog the audience's memory of *Part I*, which is what's fun about going to see a sequel. It's like hanging out with old friends again.'

Warehouses and wardrobe departments were searched to find props and clothing that had not been used for the four years in between the films. Frames from the first movie were enlarged for production designer Rick Carter to re-create the look of the movie in minute detail. The gymnasium of the First United Methodist Church in Hollywood hosted its second 'Enchantment Under the Sea'

dance, although it looked exactly like the first, with many of the same dancers returning to be part of a most unique 'revival'.

The filmmakers were also aided by the memories of the majority of the crew who returned to work on the sequels. Dean Cundey recalls an incident on the first night of filming on *Part II*. 'We were re-creating the scene where lightning struck the clock-tower, and Marty is sent back to 1985. As we were setting up the lighting, someone said, "I remember we had a light over that doorway," and another crew member recalled the exact filter that went over the light. We were able to light the scene exactly as it had been done four years ago. In most cases you have to go back and redo a job because you don't get it right the first time. We had to go back years later to redo the job because we definitely got it right the first time.'

1985

The year 1985 is the cornerstone of the Back to the Future *trilogy: where the story begins, and is ultimately resolved. In this year we are not only introduced to the characters of Marty and Doc but also to the 'character' of Hill Valley, California, as well.*

'What's happened to Hill Valley in 1985,' says Bob Gale, 'is the same thing that's happened in a lot of small towns over the years. They opened the mall in the suburbs, and that killed all the business downtown, and everything changed.'

'The changes that we made to the Hill Valley set between 1955 and 1985 reflected that suburban expansion,' adds Larry Paull. The grassy square in front of the courthouse has become a parking lot for the Department of Social Services. Some of the businesses from the '50s remain, but others, such as a pawn shop and pornographic book store, have also made their way into the neighbourhood. The Studebaker dealership now belongs to Toyota, and the malt shop is a casualty of a more health-conscious time and has been turned into an aerobics studio.

◄ *In 1985, at the Twin Pines Mall, Marty and Einstein wait for Doc Brown to unveil his latest invention.*

BIFFHORRIFIC 1985

'He's evil incarnate. And he knows it. And he's me. And I dig him.'

THOMAS F. WILSON

The altered 1985, referred to by the crew as 'Biffhorrific', is created when Old Biff travels back to 1955 to present his younger self with the Sports Almanac.

In designing the revamped Hill Valley to reflect this new glitch in the space-time continuum, Rick Carter and his fellow designers 'went wild. The Biffhorrific Hill Valley takes the common points of reference, and unleashes their "evil twins". Every lewd and greedy aspect of society is personified and showcased.'

To give these scenes their stark, foreboding look, Dean Cundey lit them using dark tones and plenty of smoke. Joanna Johnston wanted the costumes of the extras to project a seedy, aggressive persona. For the scene where Marty enters the

square to discover Biff Tannen's Pleasure Paradise Casino, 150 bikers were hired, and brought their own wardrobe. Johnston accessorized their outfits — a crucifix through the nose here, a spiked chain there, little touches that she picked up while researching punk and new wave clubs in her native London. 'The only limit to my design,' says Johnston, 'was what might be acceptable to a family audience.'

Biff's penthouse set allowed the design team to indulge in a cornucopia of glitz, trash and overall bad taste. Although not seen on camera, many small touches, like pictures of Biff with Jimmy Hoffa, and various awards from civic groups to Biff for his work in toxic waste, added greatly to the ambience.

▲ *In this 1985, where the high school burned down six years ago, former (James Tolkan) principal Strickland still thinks Marty looks like a slacker.*

▶ *Adjacent to his casino is the Biff Tannen Museum, where a video preview trumpets, 'You know the legend. Now meet the man!'*

'We had a lot of fun creating Biffhorrific 1985. We were able to be as sleazy as we could — all, of course, within the boundaries of good taste.'

BOB ZEMECKIS

2015

> *'It's a pop culture version
> of the future.'*
>
> BOB GALE

'The first thing we decided on when we were planning the future sequences,' says Bob Zemeckis, 'was that our future wasn't going to be Orwellian. We didn't want a totalitarian state where people dress in uniforms and have their heads shaved, which is actually a very easy way to depict the future in movies.' 'We also knew,' adds Bob Gale, 'that we would fail if we tried to offer real predictions of the future. We decided the only way to deal with it was to make it optimistic, and have a good time with it.'

'Although it plays a small part, our idea was not to belabour the hardware and technology. We wanted 2015 to be fun from a pop culture standpoint,' says Zemeckis. 'We went back into the past to see how far certain things had evolved into the present – which, if you think of it, is the future of the past. What we present in our future are devices and situations that are extensions of our culture.'

'It had to have a sense of reality for the audience,' continues Gale, 'because you can't identify with something that doesn't exist. We just modified ordinary, everyday conveniences. There are still TVs, only now you can watch six channels at once. There are still cars, only they can fly. Movies are still around: *Jaws 19* ("This time it's

▲ In 2015 Marty enters the Cafe '80s, which is, according to Doc, 'one of those nostalgia places, but not done very well'. The cafe's previous incarnations have been a saloon, malt shop, and aerobics studio.

◄ Original costume design sketch – 'I found the prospect of designing the clothing of the future a terrifying one, since Bob's concept had no basis in anyone else's work. We were starting from scratch,' says Joanna Johnston.

really, really personal") directed by Max Spielberg is playing at the local holomax theatre.'

It was up to Rick Carter to translate the filmmakers' visions of the future into reality. 'There's a line in the script of *Part II* describing the future that says "Hill Valley has changed for the better." That's a simple line to write, but when it came to actually building the town square, it had to be designed so the audience would immediately get that feeling upon seeing the image. Bob Z. explained that the people of the future had become more conscious of the environment and ecology, and I felt that town square should reflect that awareness. To balance out the references to commercial outlets, I introduced a strong sense of nature to turn the town square into a place where you'd enjoy sitting and watching people.'

To accomplish his task, Carter had a 60×80ft (18×24m) piece of the square excavated, filled with more than 80,000 gallons (363,000 litres) of water, and surrounded by a variety of tropical foliage. The end result of his labours found a glistening pond in the middle of the square, complemented by waterfalls and lush greenery. Asked about the look of the square, Zemeckis remarked, 'It's a true example of how the more things change, the more they stay the same. In *Part I* the 1955 square had a beautiful, grassy park. In the '80s it was paved over for a parking lot, and in 2015, once again, we have this serene park and pond – with 75 shops underneath.'

Joanna Johnston used bright, 'but not fluorescent' colours, and a vast array of fabrics to create outfits for the cast, as well as over 150 extras. As the times have changed, and the future has become a truly equal society for men and women, Johnston felt no qualms about a fashion style that was 'absolutely sexist. Men look like men, and women look like women.'

'No one knows what the future will be like,' says Neil Canton, 'but we are talking about having a reunion in 2015 to see how close we were.'

◄ Stephanie E. Williams and Mary Ellen Trainor portray Hill Valley's Finest, Officers Reese and Foley. Zemeckis and Gale have used the names Reese and Foley to identify any police officer or government agent in every script they have written together.

Standard issue for the officers of the Hill Valley Police Department.

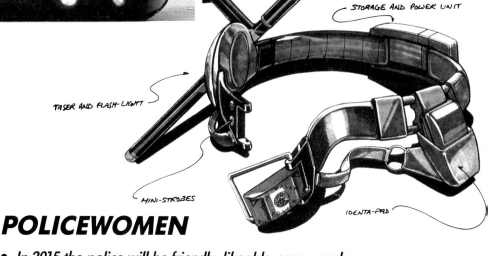

NIGHTSTICK

STORAGE AND POWER UNIT

TASER AND FLASH-LIGHT

MINI-STROBES

IDENTA-PAD

POLICEWOMEN

• In 2015 the police will be friendly, likeable, sexy – and women. Bob Zemeckis wanted them to be so attractive that people wouldn't mind being arrested.
• They are dressed in heightened police blue, with jodhpurs and short sleeves, which flatter the feminine line, yet retaining a modicum of authority.
• Their caps seem to be fairly conventional, except for the high-tech addition of an electronic readout on the hatband. The messages are quick, but if you look closely enough, you might pick up messages such as: 'Do you know where your children are? Look before you gleek! Do not covet thy neighbour's thumb! [In the future, thumbprints are an alternate form of currency.] Have you bought your tickets to the policeman's ball?'

SELF-LACING SHOES

- *Marty's amazing self-lacing sneakers were developed in conjunction with Nike.*
- *The idea originated with a piece of action that never made it to the production stage – Bob Z conceived a slam-ball game in an anti-gravity magnetic field. The shoes lit up when they touched the game floor and entered that field. The cost of the proposed scene proved to be prohibitive but the shoes remained.*
- *Shooting the automatic lacing effect was actually a simple, real-time process. Instead of one lace, the shoes had six of them, with loops that went through the sole of the shoe and through the ground. Seemingly the surface of the alley, the ground was actually a raised platform under which the special effects men pulled the loops tight as Michael J. Fox stepped into the shoe.*

FINGER LOOPS

POWER BAND
NEON LOGO

POWER LACES

SOCK TYPE CONSTRUCTION

COMPUTER
LIGHTS

GROWING AIR BAGS

ADJUSTABLE CLOTHES

- *In the future, clothes are truly one-size-fits-all, because when you touch a button, the garment conforms to the shape of the body. The idea of self-adjusting clothes came to Joanna Johnston when she was trying to solve the problem of designing a jacket that fitted Marty perfectly, yet projected the slovenly, disordered image of Marty Jr.*
- *The jacket had four areas on each side that were adjustable. Paul Brown, an English rubber specialist who worked on Batman's cape, moulded the rubber to Johnston's requirements, making it flexible and giving it the appearance of ordinary clothing material. Forty cables ran down through the jacket and down the legs of Michael's jeans. When Doc pressed the pad, six technicians pulled on the various cables to make the zipper zip, the sleeves shorten, and the epaulettes conform to Marty's body.*
- *A second jacket was designed with a 'self-drying' mode, which contained an inner bladder. Air tubes connected to the jacket inflated the garment, drying it and Marty's hair at the same time.*

▶ *Marty applies his 1985 skateboarding acumen to the 2015 hoverboard in an attempt to escape from Griff and his gang. He is ultimately victorious in his battle against the youths and successfully alters the path of his children's future destinies. As a matter of course, Marty takes the hoverboard with him when he and Doc return to 1985. What Marty doesn't know is that the futuristic hoverboard will also eventually benefit the lives of his ancestors when he travels back to 1955, and later, 1885.*

BACK TO THE
DRAWING BOARD

E VERY FILM, no matter how successful, has scenes that were cut, concepts that were rejected, and changes made for other countries, as well as television. The following pages are a small sample of ideas, illustrations and alterations that reflect the development and growth of a film from inception to release.

● *In the very first draft of the original* Back to the Future, *the 1955 Doc has a colleague who suggests a research venture with a corporation that Doc refers to as 'X-Rox'. 'Well, if it's pronounced "Zerox", why don't they spell it with a "Z"?' asks the befuddled Doc.*

STEVEN SPIELBERG Presents

BACK TO THE FUTURE

A ROBERT ZEMECKIS film

He was never in time for his classes...
He wasn't in time for his dinner...
Then one day... he wasn't in his time at all.

"BACK TO THE FUTURE" starring MICHAEL J. FOX
CHRISTOPHER LLOYD · LEA THOMPSON · CRISPIN GLOVER
Written by ROBERT ZEMECKIS & BOB GALE Music by ALAN SILVESTRI Produced by BOB GALE and NEIL CANTON
Executive Producers STEVEN SPIELBERG KATHLEEN KENNEDY and FRANK MARSHALL
Directed by ROBERT ZEMECKIS

Coming soon to a theatre near you.

▶ *The final poster for Part I. See the following pages for other versions that were not approved.*

▲ *In a scene cut from the original film, Marty is further astonished to peer into a classroom and find his mother cheating in an exam.*

▶ *Seen for the first time anywhere, this photograph shows Eric Stoltz in the role of Marty McFly. Weeks later, the same scene was reshot, as Michael J. Fox assumed the role.*

● *While in production, some scenes are filmed twice: one for the theatrical release, the other for television. While Marty might ask 'What happens to us in the future, Doc? Do we become assholes?' in the theatre, on television he is required to ask 'Do we become jerks?', a question deemed more appropriate for a family audience.*

17-year-old Marty McFly got home early last night.
30 years early.

● In 1885 Marty makes a casual reference to the movies. Of course, none of his listeners pay much attention to him, except for a little boy who asks what a movie is. Before Marty has a chance to answer, the boy is led away by a man who tells him, 'Move along, D.W., move along.' Another bystander observes, 'That little Griffith boy, can't hold him down.'

● Translation into foreign languages also poses problems. In Italy and Spain, Calvin Klein clothing is not commonly known, so the alias that Marty goes under in 1955 was changed to Levi Strauss; in France he became Pierre Cardin. Also, at the time of the first film's release, Italian television had not yet adopted the practice of airing repeat showings of series, so there was no Italian word for rerun. In 1955, when Marty is having dinner with the Baines family, instead of telling them that he saw the first-run episode of The Honeymooners they're watching, on a rerun, he claims to have seen it on a videocassette.

▲ There were a number of poster artworks done by artist Drew Struzan before the final poster was approved. Here are a number of ideas that were not used.

FILM CREDITS

PRINCIPAL CAST

Marty McFly
Marty McFly Junior
Marlene McFly
Seamus McFly .... MICHAEL J. FOX*
Dr. Emmett Brown .... CHRISTOPHER LLOYD*
Clara Clayton .... MARY STEENBURGEN[3]
Lorraine Baines McFly
Maggie McFly .... LEA THOMPSON*
Biff Tannen
Griff
Buford "Mad Dog" Tannen .... THOMAS F. WILSON*
Jennifer Parker .... CLAUDIA WELLS[1]
ELISABETH SHUE[2,3]
George McFly .... CRISPIN GLOVER[1]
JEFFREY WEISSMAN[2,3]
Dave McFly .... MARC McCLURE[1,3]
Linda McFly .... WENDIE JO SPERBER[1,3]
Sam Baines .... GEORGE DiCENZO[1]
Stella Baines .... FRANCES LEE McCAIN[1]
Mr. Strickland
Marshall Strickland .... JAMES TOLKAN*
3-D .... CASEY SIEMASZKO[1,2]
Match .... BILLY ZANE[1,2]
Skinhead .... JEFFREY JAY COHEN*
Marvin Berry .... HARRY WATERS, JR.[1,2]
Terry .... CHARLES FLEISCHER[2]
Western Union Man .... JOE FLAHERTY[2]
Babs .... LISA FREEMAN[1,2]
Needles .... FLEA[2,3]
Griff's gang .... RICKY DEAN LOGAN[2]
DARLENE VOGEL[2]
JASON SCOTT LEE[2]
Buford's gang .... CHRISTOPHER WYNNE[3]
SEAN SULLIVAN[3]
MIKE WATSON[3]
Saloon Patrons .... DUB TAYLOR[3]
HARRY CAREY, JR.[3]
PAT BUTTRAM[3]
Bartender .... MATT CLARK[3]
Gun salesman .... BURTON GILLIAM[3]
Barbed Wire salesman .... RICHARD DYSART[3]
Hill Valley Mayor .... HUGH GILLIN[3]
Engineer .... BILL McKINNEY[3]

KEY 1 = PART I, 2 = PART II, 3 = PART III, * = ALL THREE

ACKNOWLEDGMENTS:

Special thanks to Bob Gale, Bob Zemeckis and Neil Canton, Nancy Cushing-Jones, Frank Rodriguez and the Universal Pictures photo department, Mary Anne DeSimone, and especially the cast and crew of the *Back to the Future* trilogy.

PRINCIPAL CREW

Directed by .... ROBERT ZEMECKIS*
Produced by .... BOB GALE & NEIL CANTON*
Story by .... ROBERT ZEMECKIS & BOB GALE*
Screenplay by .... ROBERT ZEMECKIS[1] & BOB GALE*
Executive Producers .... STEVEN SPIELBERG*
FRANK MARSHALL*
KATHLEEN KENNEDY*
Director of Photography .... DEAN CUNDEY, A.S.C.*
Production Design by .... LAWRENCE G. PAULL[1]
RICK CARTER[2,3]
Edited by .... ARTHUR SCHMIDT*
HARRY KERAMIDAS*
Music by .... ALAN SILVESTRI*
Costume Designer .... DEBORAH L. SCOTT[1]
JOANNA JOHNSTON[2,3]
Associate Producer .... STEVE STARKEY[2,3]
Casting by .... MIKE FENTON, C.S.A.*
JANE FEINBERG, C.S.A.[1]
JUDY TAYLOR, C.S.A.*
VALORIE MASSALAS*
Unit Production Manager .... DENNIS E. JONES[1]
JOAN BRADSHAW[2,3]
First Assistant Director .... DAVID McGIFFERT*
Second Assistant Director .... PAMELA EILERSON[1]
CARA GIALLANZA[2,3]
Second Second Assistant Director .... CARLA CORWIN[2,3]
Visual Effects Supervisor .... KEN RALSTON*
Make-Ups Created by .... KEN CHASE*
Make-Ups Applied by .... MICHAEL MILLS[2,3]
KENNY MYERS[2,3]
BRON ROYLANCE[2,3]
Art Director .... TODD HALLOWELL[1]
MARJORIE STONE McSHIRLEY[2,3]
JIM TEEGARDEN[3]
Location Manager .... PAUL PAV*
Property Master .... JOHN ZEMANSKY*
Production Controller .... BONNE RADFORD*
Production Accountant .... LEANNE MOORE*
Stunt Coordinator .... WALTER SCOTT*
Camera Operator .... RAYMOND N. STELLA, S.O.C.*
Still Photographer .... RALPH NELSON, JR.*
Script continuity .... NANCY HANSEN[1]
MARION TUMEN[2,3]
Production Sound Mixer .... WILLIAM B. KAPLAN*
Boom Operator .... EARL F. SAMPSON*
Supervising Sound Editor .... CHARLES L. CAMPBELL*
ROBERT RUTLEDGE[1]
LOUIS L. EDEMANN[2,3]
Chief Lighting Technician .... MARK D. WALTHOUR*
Key Grip .... RONALD T. WOODWARD[1]
RON CARDARELLI[2,3]
Special Effects Supervisor .... KEVIN PIKE[1]
MICHAEL LANTIERI[2,3]
Second Unit Director .... FRANK MARSHALL[1]
MAX KLEVEN[2,3]
Production Illustrators .... ANDREW PROBERT[1]
DICK LASLEY[1]
MARTY KLINE[2,3]
DAVID JONAS[2]
DAVID NEGRON, SR.[3]
SIMON WELLS[2,3]
Unit Publicist .... MARSHA ROBERTSON[1]
MICHAEL KLASTORIN[2,3]